THE HISTORY OF INSTITUTIONAL RACISM IN U.S. PUBLIC SCHOOLS

Published by Garn Press, LLC
New York, NY
www.garnpress.com

Book and cover design by Benjamin J. Taylor/Garn Press
Cover Images by Susan DuFresne

First Edition, May 2018

Library of Congress Control Number: 2018935044

Publisher's Cataloging-in-Publication Data

Names: DuFresne, Susan.
Title: The History of Institutional Racism in U.S. Public Schools / Susan DuFresne.
Description: First edition. | New York : Garn Press, 2018.
Identifiers: LCCN 2018935044 | ISBN 978-1-942146-72-8 (pbk.) | ISBN 978-1-942146-73-5 (hardcover)
Subjects: LCSH: Racism. | Race discrimination. | Social justice. | Public schools--United States. | Democracy and education. | Education--Political aspects. | BISAC: SOCIAL SCIENCE / Discrimination & Race Relations. | EDUCATION / History. | EDUCATION / Violence & Harassment. | EDUCATION / Education Policy & Reform/ General. | EDUCATION / Inclusive Education.
Classification: LCC HM671.D55 2018 (print) | DDC 371.3--dc23.
LC record available at https://lccn.loc.gov/2018935044

THE HISTORY OF INSTITUTIONAL RACISM IN U.S. PUBLIC SCHOOLS

WRITTEN AND ILLUSTRATED BY
BY SUSAN DUFRESNE

GARN PRESS
NEW YORK, NY

For my family and yours, for all children and the educators who strive to empower them – and for all those who dare to engage with the uncomfortable in the name of justice – may the love beating inside the heart of this book spill light into the dark corners of our history, igniting small fires of hope to fuel our mutual struggle towards liberation together, to that end – this book is for you.

ACKNOWLEDGEMENTS

No one can predict where this book and the banner that preceded it will travel, or what conversations will take place, what minds will be changed, what actions will occur towards the dismantlement of institutional racism in our U.S. public schools as a direct or indirect result of its creation. But without the following people, none of that would have been possible and so I wish to acknowledge the following individuals and organizations for their support of this book project.

My deep gratitude extends to Becca Ritchie, for without her generosity and friendship for her funding to purchase the paint and canvases, for sharing the work with her contacts to support the banner being hung at important events. Special thanks to Marla Kilfoyle, Priscilla Sanstead, and Melissa Tomlison and the Badass Teachers Association for without their support, this idea would not have come to life. Thank you to all the BATs who suggested the banner be reinvented through a graphic novel!

Also to Julianna Dauble, Chandra Dupuis Moon, and their beautiful children who came over one day to collaborate and paint with me as the deadline for the banner's debut grew near.

To Anthony Cody, Diane Ravitch, Colleen Wood and all of the Network for Public Education Board (NPE) for hanging the banner at the NPE's annual conference in Oakland, CA to provide a place for public viewing. Special thanks to Anthony for introducing me to Denny Taylor of Garn Press, and for supporting me through my first experience in the publishing process.

I'd like to extend a special thank you to activist and artist Jimmy Betts, and also to Bill Moyer and Eric Ross of the Backbone Campaign, for sharing their knowledge on creating artful resistance.

Thank you to the National Education Association (NEA) leadership, especially Kevin Gilbert who introduced New Business Item B committing our union to work towards ending institutional racism in our public schools, and to our members who are working towards this goal.

A special acknowledgement to all the courageous educators who work with children in public schools, resist education reforms, find ways to act in deconstructing institutional racism in our U.S. society and across the globe, and engage in the work of repairing and restoring justice to all those harmed in this important pillar of democracy – our public schools.

I also wish to thank Yohuru Williams, Sandy Grande, Wayne Au, Jesse Hagopian, Jitu Brown, Journey for Justice Alliance, the #WeChoose Campaign, the #DyettHungerStrikers, Denisha Jones, Ruth Rodriquez, Wilma de Soto, Janie White, Julian Vasquez Helig, Reverend Barber, Shoneice Reynolds and her son Asean Johnson, Rita Green, Tina Alcaraz-Andres, Zer Vue, Diane Beall, Lucero Alegre, Adam Aguilera, Awo-Okaikor Aryee-Price, Nikhil Goyal, Bob Hasegawa, Brian Jones, Freedom Johnson, Hyung Kyu Nam, Karen Jennings-Lewis, Jose Vilson, Malcom London, Kenzo Shibata, Mike Hutchinson, Nikkita Oliver, Pamela Sepulveda Wilson, Paul Cheoketen Wagner, Pedro Noguera, Sergio Flores, Shawna Moore, Sherick Hughes, Tanaisa Brown, Xian Franzinger Barrett, and Tikeila Rucker. And a special thank you to all of the children and families of color in my years of teaching for their positive influence in forming my deep love for this fight for justice.

And to Denny Taylor, Ben, and David of Garn Press for the tremendous faith, trust, talent, knowledge, experience, and creativity they have put into publishing books of resistance including this one. The world is a better place filled with hope because of you. To all of you, I am most grateful.

Finally, I wish to acknowledge my husband, Shawn DuFresne who set up a humble table of sheetrock and supports on which I could draw and paint the canvases, who helped me prime and hang them to dry, who engineered a way to hang them at Westlake Center in Seattle, packaged them for shipping across the country for viewing and often joins me through all the hours I spend in activism in the resistance.

Let resistance to racism and actions of empowerment live in our words, actions, thoughts, and institutions.

Susan DuFresne
Author and Illustrator
Special Education and General Education Kindergarten Teacher
Badass Teacher and Eduactivist

FOREWORD

SANDY GRANDE

The idea that the American public school emerged through virtuous desire – to establish a free, universal, and non-sectarian system of education for all – is one of the first "alternative facts." Poor children, girls, non-whites, and children with disabilities were, from the beginning, excluded, marginalized, and/or segregated from school. Meanwhile, white, male and middle class children studied the Protestant Bible and a curriculum that was only "universal" in its centering of Anglo-American experience. The stated and tacit aim was social control and cultural hegemony.

These are the "uncomfortable truths" that Susan DuFresne so artfully and courageously asks us to confront in her landmark book. Her intention is not to affect anger, shame, or even contrition. Rather, like every good teacher, she aims to incite hope; to unleash *radical possibility* like a wildfire across the nation. Her dream of the possible is "radical" because it acknowledges that there is no tomorrow without a deep and abiding reckoning of yesterday – of history – and our struggles with and against (racial) oppression.

With the turn of each page, readers will not only travel through history but also be taken along on a remarkable journey of art-full resistance. We are invited to watch as the teacher becomes student, making visible what Robin D.G. Kelley identifies as the essential triumvirate of learning: Love. Study. Struggle. Susan's lessons are intended for all of us, but she speaks most directly to the beneficiaries of institutional racism at the same time she counts herself among them. In so doing, "Mrs. DuFresne" models for her students – young and old – what it means to be a good ally or what Indigenous peoples might refer to as a "good relative."

Throughout the text, it is clear that Susan walks in the footsteps of other white-teacher-allies such as Vivian Gussin Paley, Jane Elliott, Maria Montessori, and Peggy McIntosh. But, she also moves us beyond their teachings by connecting the dots between racial difference, economic inequality, and the accumulative logics of capital. As today's students and teachers face the dehumanizing effects of high stakes testing, standardized curricula and the culture of "accountability," it is critical to name the corporate actors who are consolidating power through the privatization of public schools. It is critical to connect the dots between the "education overhaul" enabled by disaster capitalism in Puerto Rico to that enacted upon post-Katrina New Orleans, and to tie all of it to the long history of profiteering and experimentation conducted on the minds and bodies of marginalized youth.

This beautiful book goes a long way toward achieving all of these aims. And, while the journey is not easy, the reader is never alone as the teacher guides with an outstretched hand and a firm but tender grip; the kind that only kindergarten teachers seem to have. Class is in session and the lesson for today is: "Love. Study. Struggle."

Sande Grande
Professor of Education and Director of the Center for the Critical Study of Race and Ethnicity (CCSRE), Connecticut College

FOREWORD

YOHURU R. WILLIAMS

As a historian of the Civil Rights and Black Power Movements I am keenly aware of the power of art, in all of its forms, to rouse interest, stir the conscience, and encourage resistance to inequality. Inspired by the need to communicate a deeper truth, the poet's words, the dancer's feet, and the artist's palette explode with an unharnessed creativity driven by a desire to educate, instigate and re-imagine. Black Panther Party Minister of Culture, Emory Douglas, for instance, used provocative illustrations in the pages of the Black Panther Party newspaper as the basis for a visual revolution, challenging not only the way people of color saw themselves, but also their oppressors, a fitting re-imagination of power dynamics as well as an invitation for the viewer to bear witness through the artist's lens, not simply to the stark realities of the present, but the possibilities of the future. The power of the graphic cartoon was not limited to the Black Power Movement.

United States Congressman and Civil Rights icon John Lewis is fond of sharing that one of the primary inspirations for him to write to the Reverend Dr. Martin Luther King and join the Civil Rights Movement was a 1958 comic book *Martin Luther King and the Montgomery Story*, which in vivid illustration told the story of Dr. King, Rosa Parks and the 1955 Montgomery Bus Boycott. Beyond a mere recounting of those events the comic was also an education tool, identifying various ways that young people could get involved with the movement following what it termed the "Montgomery Method," Nonviolent Direct-Action protest strategies derived for, and aimed at toppling segregation without losing sight of the shared humanity of the oppressor and the oppressed.

Lewis never forgot the power of those images, and in 2013 teamed with Andrew Aydin and graphic artist Nate Powell to tell the story of his own involvement in the Civil Rights Movement in the graphic novel trilogy *March* as a means of not only informing but also inspiring the next generation of activists, as he had once been inspired. Lewis's focus on connecting with youth, especially through pictures and text in their own image, is not surprising.

As children's author Deborah Wiles reminds us, "Telling stories with visuals is an ancient art". "The art and the text stand alone," she continues, "but together, they create something even better." They bring words to life and allow young people to see a reflection of themselves in the stories they convey."

Artist and educator Susan DuFresne continues that tradition in the present volume. *The History of Institutional Racism in U.S. Public Schools* is a bold look at how racism and inequality critically impact young people, but importantly, it is also an invitation for all of us to confront the stark reality of our present moment while challenging us to imagine ways to continue the work of eradicating destructive policies and practices that feed things like the school to prison pipeline which continue to crush the hopes and dreams of countless students of color in American schools. It is also an invitation for students to see themselves not merely as subjects in that story, but as major actors with the power, through education, imagination and protest, to produce a different outcome.

Like those who have come before her, DuFresne is well aware of the power of picture to mold young minds, communicating our shared humanity and underscoring our desire to exist in a world free from violence and inequality. One of those truths is echoed from advice offered in the 1958 Montgomery comic, which counseled readers that the "hardest" part of confronting inequality was not losing your own humanity in the process. "You have to help your enemy see you as human. He has to see you as a person who wants the same kind of things he wants: love, a family, a job, the respect of his neighbors."

This is also the core message of the haunting illustrations produced here. In the powerful images that highlight the humanity and suffering of students,

DuFresne's artwork is a call to action to not only remember but act on behalf of and in concert with the those with the most at stake, our nation's youth.

Readers will likely shed more than a few tears over these pages, tears that hopefully will manifest into a mighty river of indignation with the power to wash away fear and compel action in support and defense of our last greatest asset, our youth.

Yohuru R. Williams
Professor of History, Dean of the College of Arts and Sciences at the University of St. Thomas, Minnesota

PREFACE

WHAT TO EXPECT WHEN YOU READ THIS BOOK

DENNY TAYLOR

The History of Institutional Racism in U.S. Public Schools gives the reader an opportunity to participate in a deep rethinking of the historic events that have shaped U.S. public schools and American society. The book is presented in three parts.

In the Introduction, Susan DuFresne, the author and artist who created the three 15 foot canvases on which the book is based, writes of the creation of these huge graphic depictions of the history of racism in public schools in the U.S. In a conversation about the book Susan said:

> My first concern in painting the panels was for all children, for they are our future. Without demolishing institutional racism in our public schools, I see a very bleak future. As an artist and a teacher I wanted to hold hands with people viewing the historically accurate images I was creating and I imagined the conversations that might take place. Experience tells me that there is a deep sense of fairness and equity in American society, and that there are many people of every race, ethnic-

ity and gender, who can be trusted to speak out and act when presented with the institutional injustices, which frame public education in America. I want readers to know of my love for the very notion of public schooling. Without the struggle by courageous people of every race and ethnicity for equality and justice for every child in public schools we will lose the struggle for democratic ideals that we all care about so much.

In the Introduction, Susan will expand on these thoughts and take you with her in what could be described as a re-enactment of her creation of the panels.

In The Artwork the panels are presented for readers to view and read – "read" because there are statements, hand written or perhaps more accurately painted, by Susan. The task of transposing the images has been challenging. Susan was intent on painting the panels and her creative process preceded any thoughts of the panels one day being turned into a book. Fortunately Susan's creative genius has been matched by Ben Taylor's exceptional capability in designing both print and art books.

It has been both a privilege and a pleasure to be present during the design meetings in which Susan and Ben discussed the presentation of the individual paintings that make up the panels. You might be surprised – as I was – that one of the first tasks was to create 90°angles in all four corners of every painting. The task was also to find ways to create protocols for presenting paintings of many different sizes in pages of a specific size and which could not be expanded or reduced to fit the images. The conversations have been lively, collaborate, and truly caring of each other and of the very fragile and often tragic and disturbing images that the panels contain.

Literally hundreds of options that Ben created both for the presentation of the panels and for the cover were considered by Susan, Ben and I – with my participation being advisory and supportive. One of the major issues we considered was whether to include the writing in the margins of the original paintings alongside the images of the paintings in the book. The concern was that by having pages of text in between the images would change the experience of "seeing" the paintings. And so, the decision was made to create a third part of the book – which would provide the reader with an opportunity to consider the information that Susan used in the conceptualization of the images.

In The Artwork Panel Descriptions the reader will find the information Susan had presented in the margins of the paintings that make up the panels. Once again there were many discussions – always with the emphasis on making the experience of reading the information an opportunity for deep contemplation as well as encouraging action. You will find that this section also includes the images, and the design process of constructing the pages was approached in a similar way to The Artwork section.

Finally a note of thanks to Yohuru Williams and Sandy Grande for their support of the project, both Susan and Garn are grateful.

Thank you for your engagement with the book and for considering *The History of Institutional Racism in U.S. Public Schools.*

Denny Taylor
Emeritus Professor of Literacy Studies
Garn Press
New York, 2018

INTRODUCTION

THE HISTORY OF INSTITUTIONAL RACISM IN U.S. PUBLIC SCHOOLS

SUSAN DUFRESNE

Education ... is the practice of freedom, the means by which men and women deal critically with reality and discover how to participate in the transformation of their world.

– Paulo Freire

This book is intended to expose the institutional racism that is inherent in U.S. public schools, and more broadly, within American society. I recognize that these graphic depictions of the history of public schools may make some of us uncomfortable – angry and perhaps ashamed – and as an artist and first-time author, I recognize putting this work out for the public to view is a risk, but it is an act of both hope and humility for me.

The History of Institutional Racism in U.S. Public Schools unmasks what some have called "white fragility". Its content is intended to make us uncomfortable with both our history and current white complicity in the most recent iteration of corporate reforms, which many public school teachers and parents consider to be increasing segregation by sorting and separating out children of color, closing public schools in Black neighborhoods, feeding the school to prison pipeline, adding to neo-slavery, and monetizing children – with some children considered of greater financial value than others.

People of color have carried the burden of informing white people about their history for too long, while the white "dominant culture" denies and buries it. White people created the structure of racism and it is white people, whose eyes have been cloaked in denial to protect us from the weight of responsibility, who need to face the truth. And so with this book I wish to recognize the courage of people of color and their white supporters who have put their bodies on the line to resist institutional racism since its very white inception in public schools.

I recognize that this book is by no means a complete history of this racism. It is just one iteration of this disturbing aspect of our shared history, and like many artists and writers, when I look at the artwork I wonder how I created it. For me, as a unionist, activist, educator, and artist, it's a powerful story.

In the summer of 2015, I was a local union elected delegate to the Washington Education Association Representative Assembly [WEA-RA]. I also attended WEA-RA as a member of the Badass Teachers Association [BATs] and as a WA-BAT Administrator, and I had been involved in writing New Business Items [NBI's] and Resolutions, which were intended to forward the work of social justice through our unions.

In 2015, BATs were breaking ground nationally as leaders of this social justice work through the National Education Association [NEA] BAT Caucus, chaired by my dear friend, Becca Ritchie. I didn't attend NEA- RA that year, but from afar I was inspired by what was to take place next.

Early in July that summer, Kevin Gilbert, along with the NEA Board worked on spotlighting systemic patterns of inequity, racism, and educational injustice that impact our students, and this New Business Item was endorsed by the National Council of Urban Education [NCUEA], calling on NEA to work towards ending institutional racism.

Also in July of 2015 I attended the Backbone Campaign's #LocalizeThis! Action Camp – a two-week training camp on artful resistance. We were a diverse group of artists and activists from across the nation, and we began to confront ourselves and others on racism and white privilege. We completed a "privilege walk" as a group – with women and people of color finding themselves at the back of the pack. Through deep discussions we began to bridge our identity politics, coming together to create a meaningful action through art. Our culminating action was center stage at Westlake Center in Seattle with an "Elephant in the Room – Racism" action, including a memorial to people of color killed by police since the murder of Mike Brown. Photos of this memorial can be found by searching Twitter under #ICommit2 @BackboneProg.

One activist at the camp was the amazing visual artist, Jimmy Betts - who inspired me by creating "The Ongoing + 10,000 Tour of the United States #Fracking Banner" – a 55 foot traveling community action art banner. I loved the graphic novel style of storytelling Jimmy used to incite action as he traveled with the banner across the US that summer and fall. Immediately, I realized this medium could be used to tell the story of institutional racism in our public schools exacerbated by corporate education reforms, and I saved my idea and pondered what it would look like if I painted it.

Then came 2016 – the year Donald J. Trump became President.

That summer, without knowing what was coming down the pike, my husband and I took our own 8,000-mile activist trip on the Opt Out Bus from the West to the East Coast of the United States, through the heartland to the Southwest, and then north returning to the West Coast and finally back to Washington State, to encourage parents and students across the country to opt out of racist, standardized, high stakes tests. The highlight of the trip took place when we reached Philadelphia and we participated in a protest march, driving the bus through the city during the Democratic National Convention.

But by the time we got on the bus in Washington State to leave on this trip, the police shooting deaths of Alton Sterling and beloved educator Philando Castile were filling social media. Suddenly, the idea of protesting a standardized test

– albeit racist in its roots – seemed less significant to act upon. We struggled with how to reconcile what was most important. We didn't want to erase the messages of 100's of people who cared about education – but honestly time and rain were doing that for us.

We asked ourselves if we should transform the Opt Out Bus into a Black Lives Matter bus. We knew that the Save Our Schools Coalition had demonstrated on the steps of the Lincoln Memorial in D.C. earlier that summer on July 7th 2016, and that among the demonstrators were my friends, Denisha Jones, Jesse Hagopian, Asean Johnson, Ruth Rodriquez, Julian Vasquez Helig and Jitu Brown, National Director of the Journey for Justice Alliance – all people of color who, together with the Reverend Barber II, tied together institutional racism in public schools and the Black Lives Matter movement. We listened to their voices and as we climbed on the Opt Out Bus we knew we were going forward towards justice.

The Reverend Barber II told the crowd in D.C. that day, "Even if we don't succeed in righting the moral wrong, the children have to see us trying." His words were in our minds when we traveled across the country meeting public school educators, Badass Teachers, children, and activists across the nation who invited us to visit children and families in their communities. In each location we visited we gave books to children and we listened to their stories with empathy and love. And at each stop we made, the children were invited to write in their own words what's truly important to them when they go to school, and the children wrote their hopes and dreams on the Opt Out Bus – transforming it into the Black Lives Matter Bus.

We began our journey from Vashon, WA stopping first in Spokane, WA, driving East through Butte, MT, stopping in Medora, ND and my home town of Washburn, ND where the public school I attended is still filled with young children. We stopped next in St. Paul, MN where we were invited in to Philando Castile's neighborhood where we gave books to children and met their parents and teachers. We continued on to Chicago, IL where Rahm Emanuel has closed down more than 50 public schools in Black neighborhoods, then to Detroit, MI, where we met with children in a public park that had been abandoned but had been renewed by community activists who care about the neighborhoods in which the children we met live. We drove further East to Brooklyn, NY where 3rd grade children learning English came to a park and were given the first book they had ever owned.

We visited Boston, MA, then drove through New Hampshire and Vermont, then back south to Newark and Cape May, NJ, then west to Pittsburgh and Philadelphia, PA. Our trip took a turn going diagonally across the country driving through small towns and cities, stopping in Terre Haute, IN, then on to Ojo Caliente and Gallup, New Mexico, which is advertised as "The Most Patriotic Small Town in America". Ironically Gallup is also known by the FBI as one of the most dangerous cities in New Mexico. What we learned was that it is the city with the most unexplained and forgotten Native American deaths in New Mexico. We listened to stories of schools beleaguered with institutional racism and heard stories of young people locked up without hope or opportunity, their dreams deferred and their lives abandoned, lost and forgotten by the institutions that were supposed to protect and care for them. We drove on to Prescott, AZ, then through the Salton Sea in CA, on to Riverside and up through Oregon, back to Washington State where the month of "letting the children see us trying" energized us to continue the struggle the following year.

In 2017, after another year of teaching, came another opportunity for a summer of activism. This was the time when the three massive fifteen-foot canvases on which this book is based finally took shape. As a white artist awakening, I have heard from many educators of color who are social justice activists, saying to me: "Do your own research! Spend time with communities of color". I did both traveling on the Opt Out Bus and through other community and activist work. It was in 2017 that I truly began to visualize how I could represent what I had learned and felt in my heart about the connections between the millions of social justice activists in the Black Lives Matter Movement and the hundreds of thousands of educators, including BATs, the Opt Out Movement and the Network for Public Education (NPE) who are raising our consciousness about institutional racism in U.S. public schools.

At the end of July BATs were planning a conference in Seattle, and as a local WA-BAT Administrator, I volunteered to be on the action planning committee. The fall 2016 and winter 2017 Standing Rock movement was still painfully fresh in my mind. One of the most powerful emotive visual images to me was when a group of veterans apologized, asking for forgiveness from the 13 Indigenous Tribes at Standing Rock. I was filled with discomfort as I thought about the role of the military in creating institutional racism, and I realized in a deep and profound way that white teachers were also complicit in our role at the Boarding Schools and our continued implicit acceptance of it.

I visualized a very public "Restorative Justice Circle". I recalled the work of Jimmy Betts and envisioned a large graphic-novel style banner as an artful backdrop for our Restorative Justice Circle. At this point, I had no thoughts of publishing a book, but I did hope that the banner would travel the country to be viewed as a backdrop for local, state, and national Restorative Justice Circles to contribute to the work of dismantling institutional racism in public schools. It was time to take the ideas I had formed and bring them to life, but I knew this was not something I could do alone – the project needed to be shared with the educators who are in the forefront of the resistance movement.

BATs fully supported my vision of the work and we got to work organizing to fill the Circle with public school educators – Black, Brown and White educators – who are struggling to dismantle the racism embedded in our public schools. Becca Ritchie sent me home with enough money to buy the paint, brushes, and canvases, as she knew payday was more than a week away, whereas time was of the essence. With a budget of $300, the day after school got out, I began my research using the most convenient and free tools I had before me – online research. I searched historic documents, and studied graphic descriptions with the intent of uncovering incidents, legislation of oppression, and acts of resistance for the many disenfranchised groups across our nation. I kept thinking of what I had been taught when I was a child in school, which was so at odds with the narrative accounts and graphic images of racism and discrimination I was finding in my search of historic documents on the websites of the Smithsonian and National Park Services. I also searched through Indigenous, Black, Mexican-American, Hispanic, Latino and Asian documents available at historic, museum, government and university websites.

Troubled by what I learned I knew I had to dig deeper to find the truth. I wanted to paint a true history using primary source documents, images, and film that included the voices of people of color as well as historic documents that recorded events from the perspective of European ancestry, which were ignorant of bias, and for the most part, discriminatory. I studied over 180 written online resources and more than 400 visual images – including engravings from the early 1600's. In addition I conducted Internet searches for newspaper articles, photographs, and other social media sources for both historic documentation and for examples of institutional racism prevalent today. Instead of being overwhelmed by this study, I felt even more inspired to act.

I chose the graphic novel style, because it was also important that the visual work was simplistic enough to be viewed from a distance to draw the viewer in closer. However, I am not a practiced graphic novel style artist, and so I also studied this style as it has been applied in the topic of racism as well.

I chose a color palette of turquoise, yellow, orange, greens, red, brown and black – a palette similar to the one used by Jimmy Betts. The work needed to be bright, and the various images across the three 4' by 15' painter's canvases totaling 45 feet in length needed to be tied together with a common color theme. I used latex house paint, acrylic artist paints, and permanent black markers to complete the paintings after doing pencil sketches over the primed painter's canvases.

This deep research occupied my first 6 weeks of the 2017 school vacation. I began the painting process, fittingly, on July 4th, and worked continuously until the final panel was completed on July 21st. Looking back on that time it still surprises me that the entire project took only six weeks of all-consuming research and three weeks of almost round-the-clock painting. It was one of the most intense visceral, cerebral and emotive moments of my life as an artist and activist.

As I read the history of repeated incidents of oppression, I was filled with empathy and outrage for each person while at the same time as I read about their stories I felt their humanity. It is hard to put into words, which is why I consider it so important that readers have an opportunity to view the images and experience their own epiphany. My hope was (and still is) for each viewer to look at the paintings and recognize their own truth.

I want readers to be inspired by the faces I painted – by the courage of the people I have tried to represent, to know in their hearts that Black and Brown lives matter, that their experiences of institutional racism and discrimination must become a part of our collective experience, and that we have important work to do together. Freire tells us, "If you have come to help me, you are wasting your time, but if you have come because your liberation is bound up with mine, then let us work together." As long as institutional racism exists in public schools and U.S. society, only together can we be truly free.

I had a deadline to complete this work for the BAT Conference. I began to sleep, eat, and breathe this history. I created a storyboard on the canvases that depicted a rough timeline, but rather than create the entire banner, I planned only a few panels at a time, but always with the end in mind. I primed the painter's cloth canvases, then began to plan out the lettering and panels, measuring them out and sketching my work in pencil. I didn't have time to do revision after revision, thus after measuring out each panel and planning what to paint, I mixed my paints and put the work down as a first and final draft all at once. The paintings flowed out of me as I tried to tie each story to the next in history. All the while I was painting one panel, I was planning the next to build on the story, with what is happening in our public schools currently to finish it off.

Giving birth to a project like this was not without struggle. Some days I experienced painter's block. The idea for the next panel was not something I considered lightly. I knew I could not include every incident in history in the panels. It was sometimes excruciating deciding which parts to leave out. I admit that these decisions may not be the same choices that friends of color may have made, or white friends either. With the pressure of time, I was not always able to seek their advice. That said, I tried to honor all ethnicities – and their struggles for freedom in each representation – to the best of my ability.

I felt I got to know everyone that I painted and that I developed a relationship with them as I worked to bring them to life for the viewer. I began with the "discovery" and birth of our nation, and I felt on my brush the weight of history as year after year I depicted the findings of my research on the onslaught of violence, murder, humiliation, ethnic cleansing, forced assimilation, lynching, enslavement and corporal punishment, that together create a structure of institutionalized racism and oppression within our public schools.

But I also wanted to depict the fight for justice, which was there from the beginning. There have always been activists, many of them educators, ready to fight for justice in U.S. public schools. Teachers especially have always been courageous in their resistance to racism and oppression and I wanted to share this history to inspire others through the images I was painting to take up that truth and join the resistance movement.

In many ways the task I had set for myself was filled with pitfalls and I knew it would be easy for me to stumble in my portrayal of people of every race and ethnicity. As I viewed the engravings and photographs of individuals of color, I wanted to be careful in my painting, to be sensitive to paint human beings and not stereotypes, to show the emotion of the individuals, and to elicit an emotive response from those who would view this work. Thinking about the research and visual images I found the writings of Paulo Freire foremost in my mind. "No pedagogy which is truly liberating can remain distant from the oppressed by treating them as unfortunates and by presenting for their emulation models from among the oppressors," Freire writes. "The oppressed must be their own example in their struggle for redemption."

On July 22nd 2017, one day after the panels were completed, we traveled to Seattle. That evening at the BATs Conference, Marla Kilfoyle, Melissa Tomlinson, Priscilla Sanstead – Cofounders and Directors of the National BATs and the WA BATs – invited attendees to an action and we carried the banner to the Bill and Melinda Gates Foundation to express our outrage at what many feel is the irreparable damage Bill and Melinda Gates have done to the U.S. public school system. Many public school teachers and parents also believe their policies and funding of national education projects have also increased segregation and exacerbated discrimination by their promotion of charter schools and their support of the privatization of public schools. At the same time there is an increasingly common view among public school teachers that Bill and Melinda Gates – who claim "All Lives Have Equal Value" – have made the most of the school-to-prison pipeline, by investing in GEO Group private prisons, and that their use of prisoners to package Microsoft products constitutes neo-slavery.

And so, BATs marched at dusk on the Bill and Melinda Gates Foundation, holding up the banner to protest and raise consciousness of the many ways in which we consider Bill and Melinda Gates have fostered institutional racism and discrimination in U.S. public schools. I began by reading every word on the panels while Jeff Snyder, a WA BAT and Backbone Campaign activist, projected the following light messages on the side of Gates Foundation building:

> The Gates Foundation Policies Increase Institutionalized Racism in Public Schools
>
> Danger – Badass Teacher resisting corporate education reform
>
> Gates Foundation Failures Show Philanthropists Shouldn't Be Setting America's Public School Agenda

We left peacefully when the Gates Foundation security contingent demanded that we leave the property, and Marla Kilfoyle continued our reading on the public sidewalk, while Jeff Snyder continued casting projected light messages on the building.

The following day, the banner was unrolled again and on view for the public, creating a backdrop at Westlake for our Restorative Justice Circle. Those who attended the Circle were invited to sign commitments on how they would work toward dismantling institutional racism in U.S. public schools.

Traveling across the U.S. on the Opt Out Bus, participating in the resistance movement created by public school teachers, and conceptualizing and painting the panels has deepened my understanding of white privilege and my realization of how endemic structural racism is in U.S. society. I am acutely aware of the never-ending history of ethnic cleansing, enslavement, racism, and genocide of our fellow Indigenous, Black, and Brown human beings. I know I risk offending some of the white audience who may chance upon this book and are not ready to face the hard truths of institutional racism in our public schools. I know I run the risk of offending some people of color for perhaps not telling a complete enough history – for leaving something important out – or for telling this history from the very real privilege of whiteness. But I also know, as Freire wrote, "Washing one's hands of conflict between the powerful and the powerless means to side with the powerful, not to be neutral."

For the sake of the nation and all our children we cannot remain neutral. We have to face our fear, anger, denial and shame, and participate in actions that focus on restorative justice and reconciliation. With unbreakable resolve we must ensure for all our children a more egalitarian future in which every child is cherished and nurtured, attends a public school that receives the sufficient funding it needs for every public school child to receive the very best education possible, regardless of race, gender, ethnicity or religion. Only then will we live in a democratic society in which restorative justice is used to eradicate racism so that all children can thrive. The artwork panels follow next in their entirety and without interruption.

Susan DuFresne
Vashon, WA, 2018

THE HISTORY OF INSTITUTIONAL RACISM IN U.S. PUBLIC SCHOOLS

THE ARTWORK

Every single public school is built on stolen land.

Timeline of Slavery in America: 1501 - 1865

Timeline of Slavery in America: 1501 - 1865

America's schooling regularly included corporal punishment and humiliation from the onset.
DUNCE
21. THE DUNCE.

Early schooling was intended to produce youth who would obey and could read the BIBLE. Corporal punishment was intended to drive the DEVIL from the child's body.

1703-
1711

as illegal to teach
ved Africans to
and
in the
h.

5% became literate
at great person
risk!

DUNCE

Indian Removal Act - 1830
· 15,665 people of Cherokee Nation memorialize Congress in PROTEST.
· Outraged citizens join to protest across U.S.
1838
Trail of Tears
Thousands died.
(Estimated 4,000+)

1864-Navajo Long Walk
Estimated 2,380 died.
8,500+ men, women, and children forced off their land - marched and held by military in internment camp for four years

in PROTEST.
to protest across U.S.

Thousands died.
(Estimated 4,000+)

Indian Remova
·15,665 people
memorialize
·Outraged citize
183
Trail of
Tears

ct - 1830
Cherokee Nation
ress in PROTEST.
join to protest across U.S.
Thousands died.
(Estimated 4,000+)

1864-Navajo

Estimated 2,3

8,500+ men, w
children forced
land-marched and
military in inter

ng Walk
ed.
en, and
heir
d by
nt
for
r
years

Indian Boarding Schools used abuse

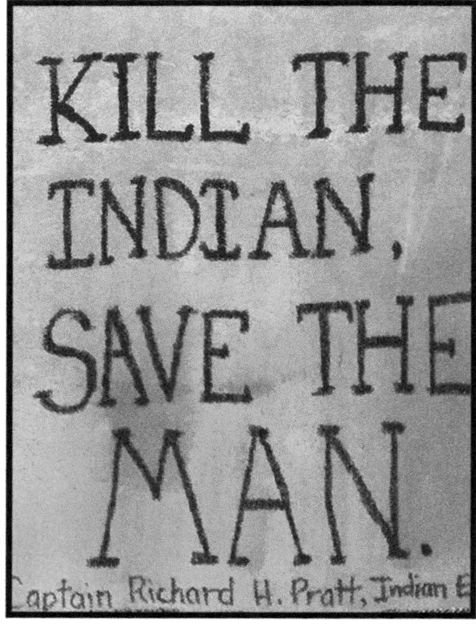
KILL THE INDIAN, SAVE THE MAN.
Captain Richard H. Pratt, Indian E

Indian Boarding School often had small jail

Navajo - Before

Tom Turtino - After

Long braids were cut off. New white names were assigned. Military-like uniforms were issued. Some were beaten with boards until their back was broken for speaking their Native language.
25 BIA schools by 1902-6,000. By 1973-60,000. Those who died? Thousands!

RSTUV
WXYZ
B
A
cat

For a brief period, some schools were integrated.

African Americans organi
education to their
in the South.

to bring
ren

For a brief period, some schools were integrated.

"Mexican Americans have lower levels of education than non-Hispanic Whites and Blacks. Some scholars have argued that this is a result of Mexican immigrants having relatively low levels of education especially by standards in the United States, yet this gap is persistan and continues into the fourth generation (Telles & Ortiz, 2008). To explain this, we have argued that the education disadvantage for Mexican Americans largely reflects their treatment as a stigmatized racial group rather than simply being a result of low immigrant human capital or of other causes suggested in the literature. (Telles & Ortiz, 2008). -NCBI

Note: Mission schools most often resulted in cultural and linguistic genocide

Common Schools moved West 1840-1850 - Public schools aided in cultural and linguistic genocide, clashing with the values of Mexican Americans.
Anglo parents often insisted on segregation to protect white children from being schooled with the "dirty and diseased." -NPS

Common Schools:
Horace Mann argued all citizens, regardless of race or economic status, shoul[d] have equal access to a tuition-free, tax support[ed] public school system to achieve the unshackled status of a true DEMOCRACY. -
Boston State Univ.

• Texas Rangers killed hundreds -or thousands of Mexican Americans between 1915-1919.

• Lynching was common between 1860-1960, more than 4,000 African Americans were lynched between 1877-1950. Native Americans, Mexican Americans, and Asians were also lynched-as well as whites who helped Blacks.

Maintaining Oppression

Chinese Must Go!
• 1853 - Chinese children locked out of public education. 1st Presbyterian Church opens for them 1869. - Pressreader San Francisco
1927 - Gong Lum v. Rice Supreme Court rules Chinese as non-white for segregation in public schools.

Comm
Ho
argu
rega
econ
have
tuition-
public s
achieve
status o
DEM
Bo

1927 - Gong Lum v. Rice
Supreme Court rules
Chinese as non-white
for segregation in
public schools.

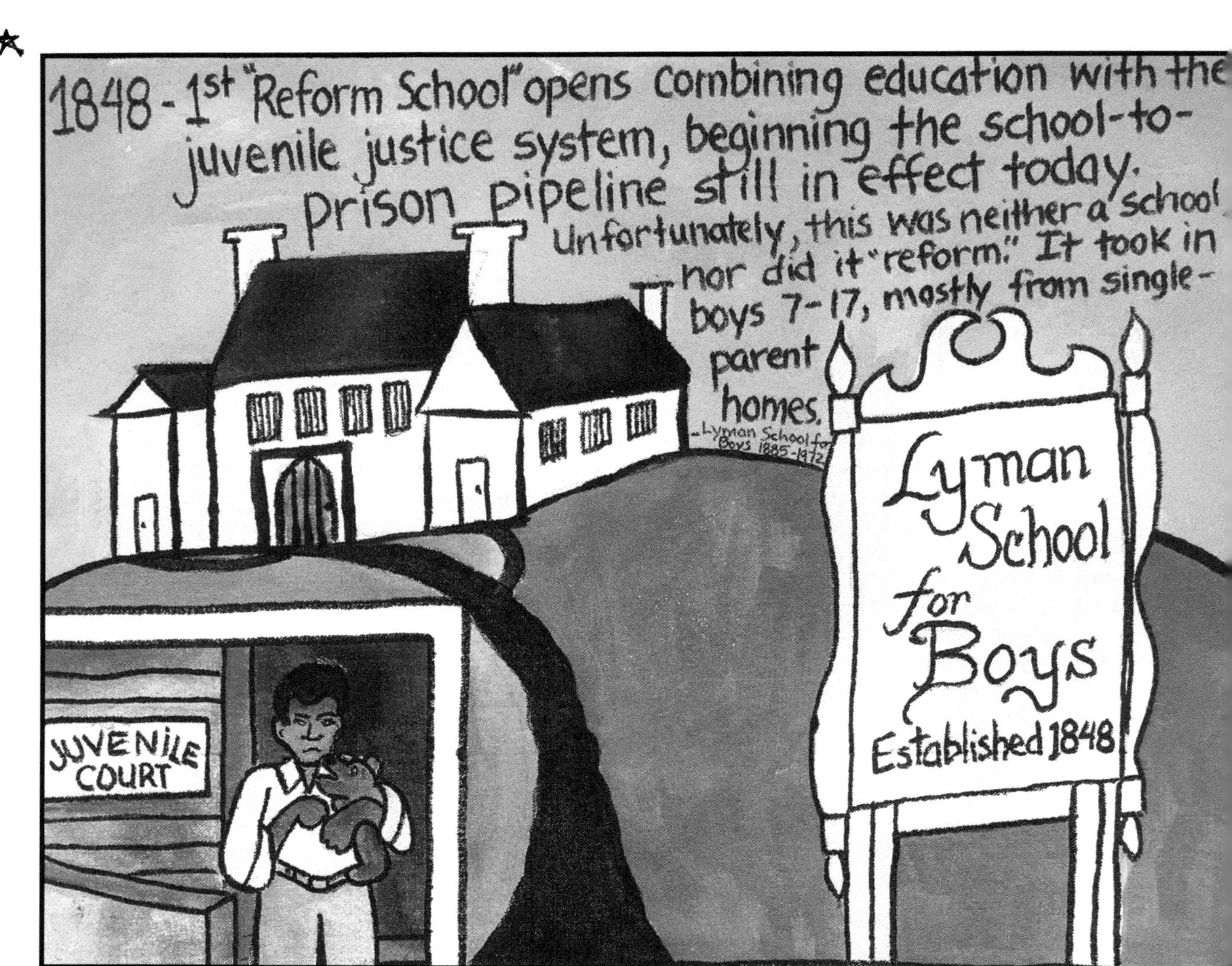
1848 - 1st "Reform School" opens combining education with the juvenile justice system, beginning the school-to-prison pipeline still in effect today.
Unfortunately, this was neither a school nor did it "reform." It took in boys 7-17, mostly from single-parent homes.
-Lyman School for Boys 1885-1972
Lyman School for Boys
Established 1848
JUVENILE COURT

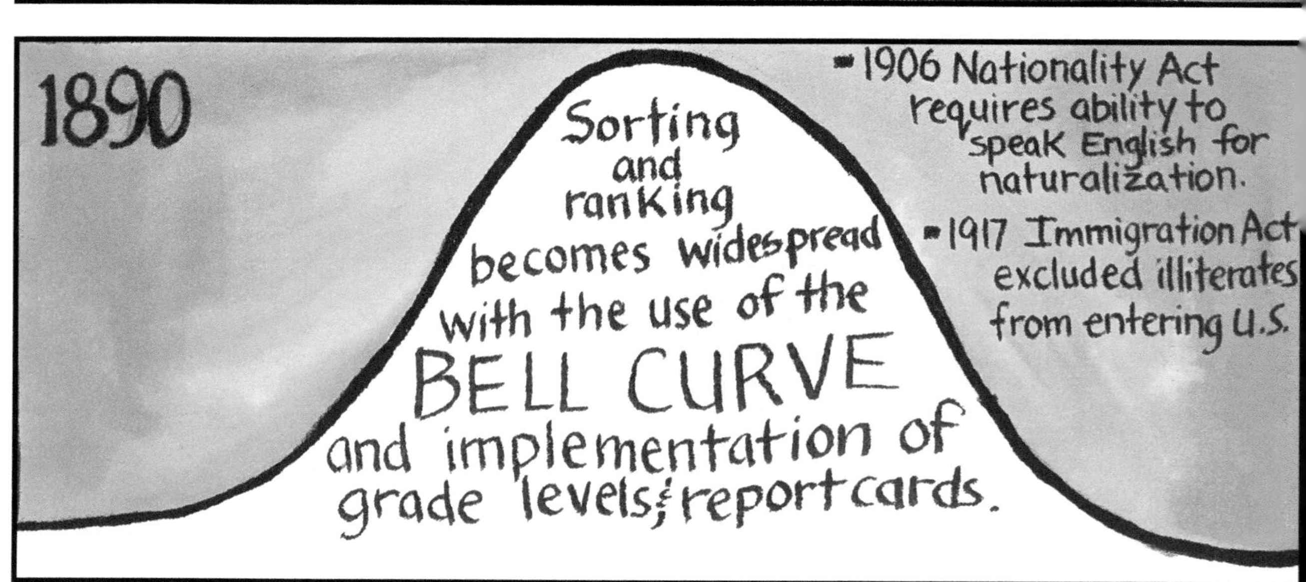
1890
Sorting and ranking becomes widespread with the use of the BELL CURVE and implementation of grade levels & report cards.
• 1906 Nationality Act requires ability to speak English for naturalization.
• 1917 Immigration Act excluded illiterates from entering U.S.

Eugenics Used to Justify

STERILIZATION:

1849 - 1st proposed in Texas, Gordon Lincecum through 1981 - Oregon performs last sterilization.

1927 - Buck v. Bell led to at least 70,000 forced steril. *

EUG

nics

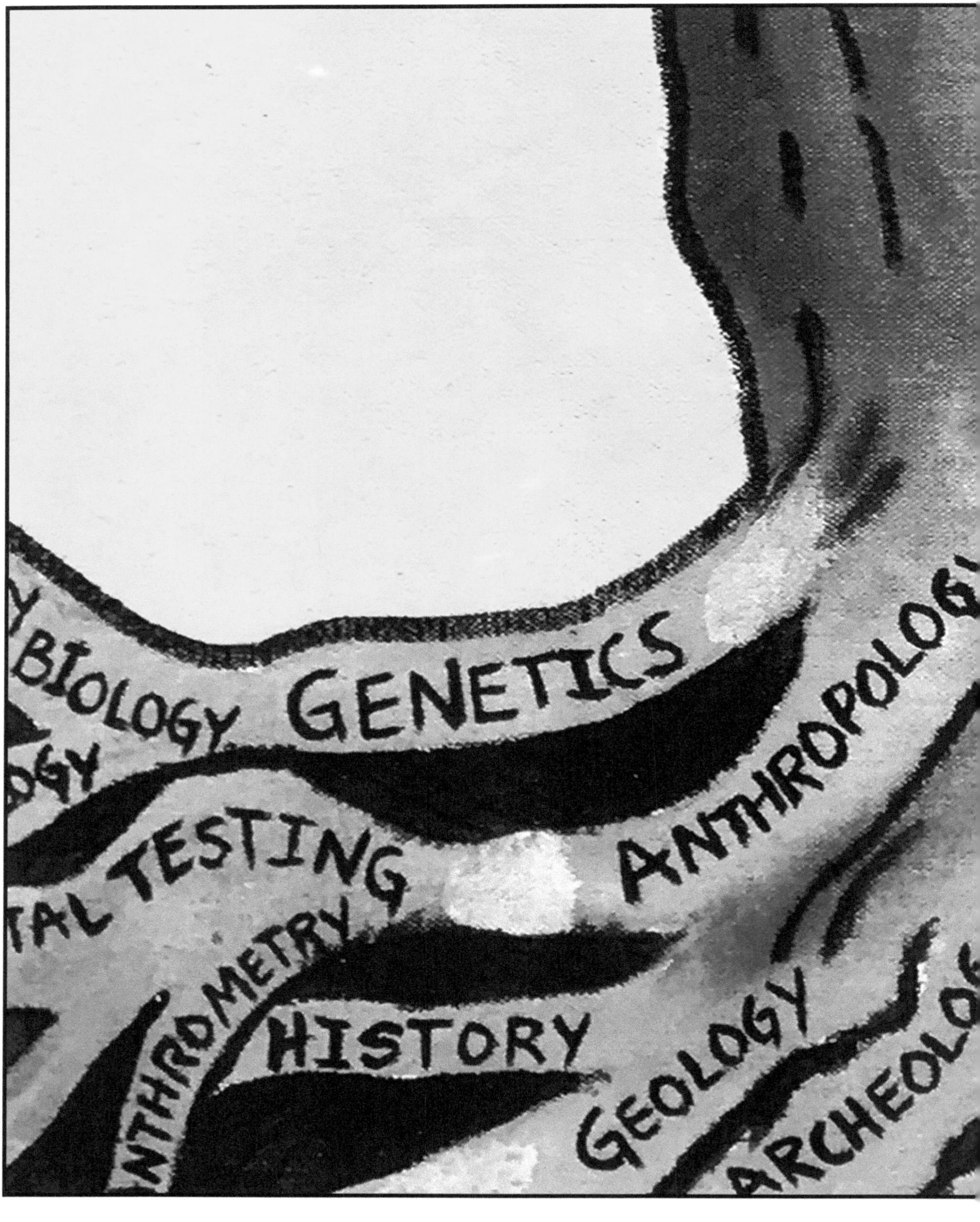

BIOLOGY
GENETICS
TESTING
HISTORY
GEOLOGY

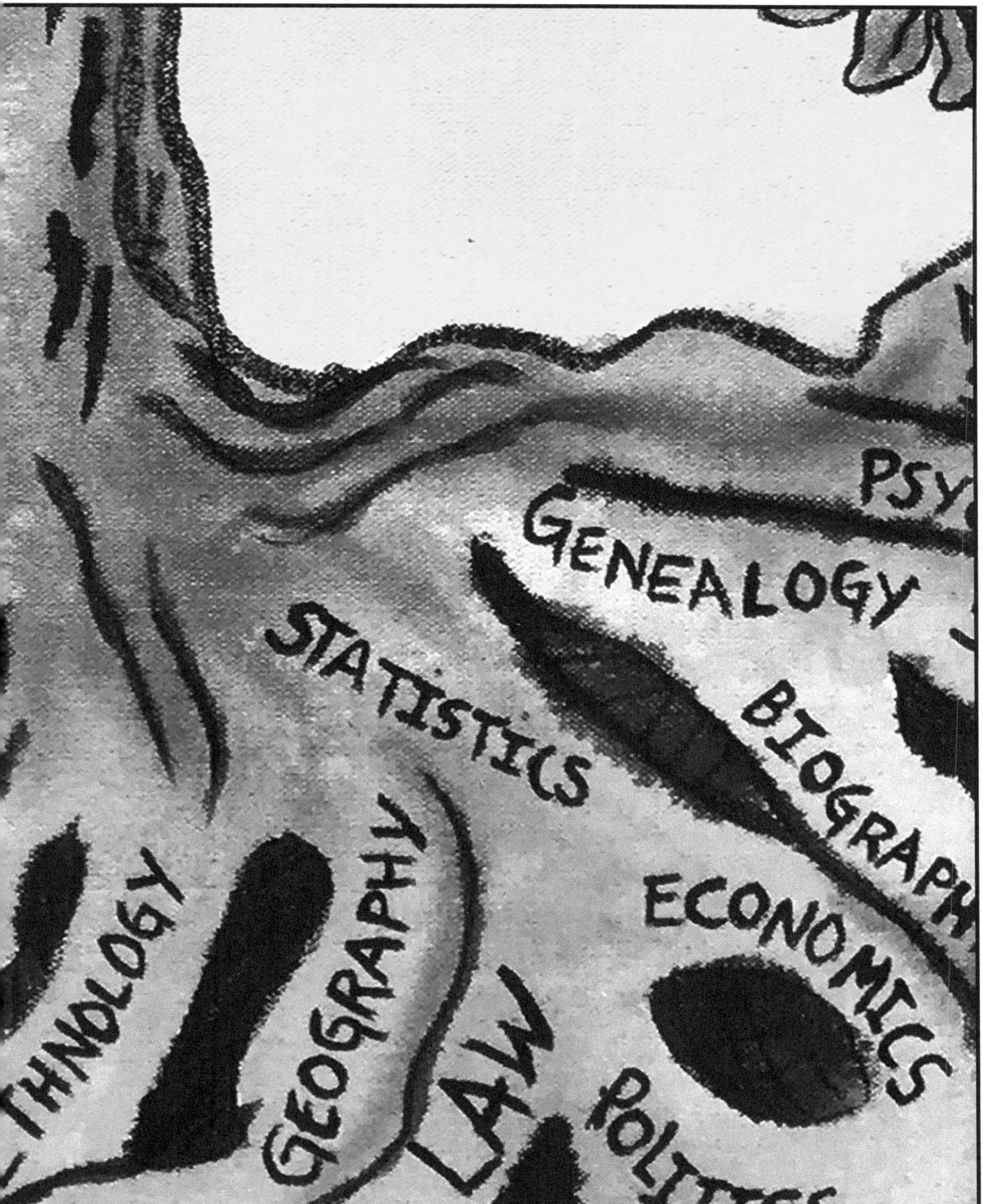

GENEALOGY
STATISTICS
ECONOMICS
GEOGRAPHY
LAW

Lewis Terman launched study: Genius & Stupidity: A Study of the Intellectual Processes of Seven "Bright" and Seven "Stupid" Boys. He administered tests in English to Spanish-speakers and non-schooled African Americans, concluding: "High-grade or border-line deficiency... is very common among Spanish-Indian and Mexican families of the Southwest and also among negroes. Their dullness seems to be racial, or at least inherent in the family stocks from which they come... Children of this group should be segregated into separate classes." (Terman, 1916, p. 91-92) Terman added: "They constitute a grave problem because of their unusually prolific breeding." ★

MERITOCRACY
TECHNOCRACY
PHILANTHROPY
CLASS A
CLASS B
CLASS C
EDUCATION
INTELLIGENCE TEST
SCHOOL $
Rockefel
Carnegie
Rockefeller
and Carnegie,
like Bill Gates,
Eli Broad, and the
Waltons, Kochs
used their wealt
to radically bend
the public educati
system in ways to
sort, rank, and cul
children of color.

↳ how?

Rockefeller
SCHOOL
$
Rockefeller and Carnegie, like Bill Gates, Eli Broad, and the Waltons, Kochs

were school-age children,
infants,

and young adults not yet of voting age." —
Years of Infamy, Michi Weglyn

While in captivity, they were forced to pledge allegiance

•1930-1950 - NAACP bring series of suits over unequal pay for Blacks and whites in South.
•1933 - NAACP begins legal campaign to desegregate education.
•1935 - SC requires school bus drivers to be same race as students.
•1945 - Southern consensus - "An educated "boy" could become a danger.
•1946 - Mendez v. Westminster desegregates CALIFORNIA - Mexican Americans
•1949 - 17 states enacted laws requiring racial segregation of public school children.
•1954 Brown v. Board of Ed.
•1960 - Ruby Bridges

SOUTH IS POOR
SEGREGATION
will Make IT
POORER
SEGREGATION
IS RACISM!
But
DEMOCRACY
NAACP
Little
Rock
Nine

1969–"A National Tragedy" report on Native American Boarding Schools. Billy Wright says he still has nightmares from years of abusive discipline and that he and many other former students were traumatized into recreating this harsh environment for their own families. "You grow up with discipline, but when you grow up and you have families, then what happens? If you're my daughter and you leave your dress out, I'll knock you through that wall. Why? Because I'm taught discipline." –Billy Wright

Charla Bear—NPR (2008)

FREEDOM

not taught in school

1971- Ten school buses bombed by KKK -Pontiac, MI
SOUTHERN WHITES ARE THE NEGROE'S BEST FRIENDS BUT NO INTEGRATION

Forced bussing, forced integration was met with violence, massive resistance
STOP

1974 -U.S. Supreme Court rules in Lau v. Nichols - school districts MUST provide bilingual education or remedial English classes.

1974 Boston Riots over forced bussing, integration
The City has NO CLASSROOM FOR My Child

Valerie Banks was the ONL student to show up on 1st day of geography at South Boston HS.
1974
Whites Boycott RIOT rather th integrat

Indian Child
Welfare
Act

1983- A NATION AT RISK

2001-
No Child Left Behind

2005- "I think the best thing that happened to the education system in New Orleans was Hurricane Katrina." - Arne Duncan, US Sec. of Ed.
TAKE-OVER BY R S D
"No Excuses" Charter Schools
No textbooks, desks,
Microwaved frozen meals,
Militarized Security outnumbering TEACHERS
SCHOOL BUS

2009- Race to ? the Top ???
For whom ?
REWARD
PUNISH
Trauma
Biased Testing
Biased Curriculum
Poverty
Language
Racism

2005- "I think the best thing that happened to the education system in New Orleans was Hurricane Katrina." - Arne Duncan, US Sec. of Ed.

TAKE-OVER BY

R S D

"No Excuses" Charter Schools:

No textbooks, desks,

Microwaved frozen meals,

Militarized Security outnumbering TEACHERS

SCHOOL BUS

No Chil

Left Behind

SCHOOL SURVEILLANCE
COMMON CORE
Smarter Balanced
PARCC
Sorry, all ART, PE, Music, Sports, Field Trips CANCELLED DUE TO TESTING
PUBLIC SCHOOL
Library Closed Testing
SBA
ZERO TOLERANCE CHARTER
PRISON PREP
Stigmatized
Segregated
Silenced
Surveilled
Broad School Closure Manual

PRIVATIZATION OF PUBLIC SCHOOLS AND THE PRISON SYSTEM LEADS TO UNREGULATE VIOLENCE.
PRIVATE ELITE SCHOOLS
WHITE FLIGHT CHARTER SCHOOLS
WHITE FLIGHT CHARTER SCHOOLS
WHITE FLIGHT CHARTER SCHOOLS
HIGH SES PUBLIC SCHOOLS
HIGH SES PUBLIC SCHOOLS
HIGH SES PUBLIC SCHOOLS
HIGH SES PUBLIC SCHOOLS
HIGH SES PUBLIC SCHOOLS
LOW SES PUBLIC SCHOOLS
LOW SES PUBLIC SCHOOLS
LOW SES PUBLIC SCHOOLS
LOW SES PUBLIC SCHOOLS
LOW SES PUBLIC SCHOOLS
DEFUNDED STATE OR MAYORAL TAKEOVER Public Schls
DEFUNDED STATE OR MAYORAL Takeover Public Schls
DEFUNDED STATE OR MAYORAL TAKEOVER Public Schls
DEFUNDED STATE OR MAYORAL TAKEOVER Public Schls
DEFUNDED STATE OR MAYORAL TAKEOVER Public Schls
DEFUNDED STATE OR MAYORAL TAKEOVER Public Schls
ZERO TOLERANCE CHARTER SCHOOLS
ZERO TOLERANCE CHARTER SCHOOLS
ZERO TOLERANCE CHARTER SCHOOLS
ZERO TOLERANCE CHARTER SCHOOLS
ZERO TOLERANCE CHARTER SCHOOLS
ZERO TOLERANCE CHARTER SCHOOLS
ZERO TOLERANCE CHARTER SCHOOLS
examples ?
PRIVATE PRISON
Shoot!
Sentenced
U.S. 80 Youth Prisons
U.S. 5% World Population 25% of Worlds Prisoners
U.S. Prison Population increased 500% in 30 years
U.S. 1/108 adults was in prison or jail in 2012.
U.S. 1/28 children has a parent behind bars
U.S.
BLACK STUDENTS REPRESENT 31% OF SCHOOL RELATED ARRESTS
POLICE MURDERS
68% of all males in state/Fed prison do not
Native Americans are more likely to be killed by police
2016 10.13 million Native Amer.
40% of students expelled from U.S. schools are
2016 6.66 million Blacks
Native American Youth are 30% more likely to be referred to juvenile court.
POLICE MURDERS
2016 3.23 million Hispanic Latino
For every 100 students suspended, 15 were black, 7.9 were Americ. Indian, 6.8 were Latino and 4.6 were
Black Students are 3.5 times more likely to be suspended
2016 2.9 million Whites
POLICE MURDERS
Asian 1.17 million 2016
1 out of 6 Latino males will be incarcerated in life
9% Asian-Pacific Islanders-incarceration rate low-because they are classified
TAX

Allusion / Deception

Personalized Learning
Sec rity will be enforced for ALL mis behavior!
BLOCKS and LEGOS
DRAMATIC PLAY
DATA ENTRY CLERK
Microwave YOUR OWN LUNCH KIDS!
GEARS
We Shall Overcom
Martin's Big Words

THE ARTWORK PANEL DESCRIPTIONS

"We approach the radical imagination not as a thing that individuals possess in greater or lesser quantities but as a collective process, something that groups do and do together through shared experiences, languages, stories, ideas, art, and theory."

Alex Khasnabish and Max Haiven

Imagine a sheet rock table set up in an unfinished room in a daylight basement with one of three massive 15x4 feet canvases rolled out and ready for me to paint graphic representations of the first 500 years of the history of racism and discrimination in public schools in the United States. It's an enormous challenge. I have sketched the images on the canvases and I've opened the cans of latex paint and tubes of acrylic artist paint, and I've sorted my paintbrushes and gathered masses of permanent black makers. I am ready to start painting.

Looking back I recognize this was a moment of "radical imagination" – which Alex Khasnabish and Max Haiven describe as "the basis of solidarity and the struggle against oppression, which is the key to building robust, resilient, and powerful movements." It sounds like such a momentous idea but actually it's not. Radical imagination begins with a blank canvas on a table, and a public school teacher who is a self-taught artist poised to paint historical depictions of the abuse and mistreatment of children in public schools because of their race, ethnicity, religion and country of origin.

Looking back, I admit that the findings of my research made me angry and at times made me cry. But even in the moments when my emotions were raw, I knew my task was not only to paint truthful and uncensored historical pictorial images, but also to grow in empathy and wisdom. I knew, even then, that through radical imagination my task was to join with so many other educators who are activists and who struggle together for social justice for every child, and to encourage conversations about institutional racism and discrimination that can lead to radical transformations in US public schools.

Painting the panels became all-consuming, and when I had more ideas than I could fit in the paintings I quickly picked up a marker and jotted the research notes that I did not want to forget around the edges of my paintings. At that time I was not thinking that my panels would be transformed by Garn Press and published as a book. In our design meetings the big question was how we could make sure that my notes painted in the margins were not lost when the panels were turned into a book.

In the following pages I will continue to share my thinking as I painted, and you will find my margin notes. My goal is to model the possibilities of radical imagination that I experienced when I was painting the panels, to encourage you to undertake your own projects and activities that inspire in you similar imaginations of a just and empathetic society in the belief that the future is up to us.

Every single pub
school is built on stolen land.

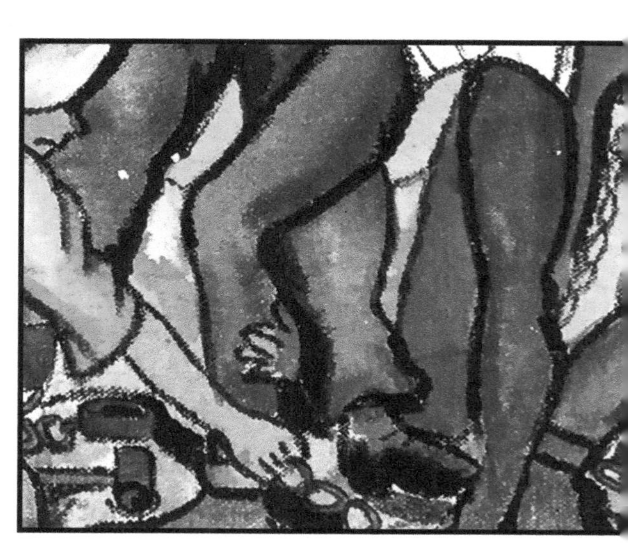

“

You can’t hold a man down without staying down with him.” - Booker T. Washington

PANEL ONE: SLAVERY - THE ROOTS OF OPPRESSION LIVE ON

When I was drawing this panel I found myself thinking about the colors I would use when I started painting. I wanted the images I was creating to connect all of us – you and me – with the lives of all those who had been captured and enslaved. My hope was that this panel would encourage you to delve more deeply into this period in U.S. history. As I worked I kept thinking about the seizure of the land belonging to Indigenous people, and I wondered how taking the lands of Native Americans and their enslavement impacts U.S. society today. I thought too of the African men, women and children who were brought to America and enslaved. The Southern Poverty Law Center has raised the concern that even today public school students still do not study slavery or consider how racism and discrimination impact the lives of children and their families. With a marker I wrote the following notes in the margins of the first panel.

My Research Notes in the Margins of the First Panel:

- Enslavement of Indigenous people, Native Americans, murder and disease enabled the colonizers to seize land.

"The Southern Poverty Law Center has raised the concern that even today public school students still do not study slavery or consider how racism and discrimination impact the lives of children and their families."

- Enslavement of Africans enabled profit as well.
- Oppressive schooling became possible via acts of terror.

Your Research Notes

I wonder what kinds of reactions you have to the paintings, and also to my research notes? Can you imagine being a Native American or African man, women or child in one of these scenes? What notes would you have written in the margins if you were painting these panels?

Possible Actions

Hundreds of years of history have brought us to the present time when racism and discrimination still exist. Do we have any alternative other than to act? If you are comfortable sharing your thoughts – for many different reasons you might not want to share them and that's okay – perhaps your first action might be a conversation in your high school, college or local community about what actually happened in America's first century. Of course, you will come up with many ideas for action on which you can work together to encourage solidarity. For example, using the concept of radical imagination you might create locally meaningful ways to share this history and to act in solidarity on projects to achieve restorative justice and reconciliation.

America's schooling regularly included corporal punishment and humiliation from the onset.
DUNCE
21. THE DUNCE.

“

It is easier to build strong children than to repair broken men.”

- Frederick Douglass

PANEL TWO: THE DUNCE

I found the early engraving entitled "The Dunce" in *The New England Primer*– a children's book used to teach the alphabet and religion in early Puritan schools. I studied the image on my cellphone and began sketching. Two hundred years ago the drawing of "The Dunce" provided a rationale for the use of corporal punishment, but the image was also used as a deterrent. On the engraving of the child portrayed as "The Dunce" it states, "This is a sight to give us pain. Once seen ne'er wished to see again." The irony was not lost on me. As I dipped my brush in the paint I thought about the use of corporal punishment and shaming still prevalent in U.S. public schools in many states today. In the margins of the panel I jotted the points I wanted to remember.

My Thoughts Painted in the Margins of the First Panel:

- 1600s-2017 – In 19 States, mostly in the South, Southwest, and Midwest, corporal punishment remains legal, used at teacher discretion much more prevalently against children who are Black, African American, Native American and Hispanic.
- Black children are 2½ times more likely to receive corporal punishment than white children. American Indian and Alaska Natives get hit at a higher rate than others.

enabled by constraint & seclusion usually?

Your Research Notes

I am going to ask you similar questions as I asked in response to the first panel. I wonder what kinds of reactions you have to the painting of the child in a

"Two hundred years ago the drawing of 'The Dunce' provided a rationale for the use of corporal punishment, but the image was also used as a deterrent."

dunce's hat and how you feel about the teacher with a switch? Can you imagine being the child in the painting? What thoughts would you have written down if you were painting this panel?

Possible Actions

Once again, hundreds of years of history have brought us to the present time when children are still being humiliated and shamed. Possible actions? You could begin by sharing a time when you or someone you know felt humiliated or excluded by punishment in school and what other action could have been taken. Remember not everyone will want to speak. After that? Perhaps a simple letter in which you share your experiences? There's a role for writers, devisers, rhymers, dancers, and of course, painters, who could find ways to share their restorative actions with Members of Congress, legislators and educators.

1703-
1711
It w
ensla
read
write
Sou

5% became
at grea

risk!

DUNCE
ame literate
great person
risk!

“

Power is of two kinds. One is obtained by the fear of punishment and the other by acts of love. Power based on love is a thousand times more effective and permanent than the one derived from fear of punishment.” - Mahatma Gandhi

PANEL THREE: RELIGION, PUNISHMENT, AND THE DANGER OF EDUCATION

When I was painting the child in the dunce's hat I kept imagining the lives of the other children in *The New England Primer*. What happened to children who read in their school primers, "The idle fool is whipped at school"? The images and words in lessons from *The New England Primer* stayed with me. I wrote "Early schooling was intended to produce youth who would obey and could read the BIBLE. Corporal punishment was intended to drive the DEVIL from the child's body." But I also wanted to make sure the panels reflected the lives of those who took huge risks to become literate, and I also wrote on the panel, "It was illegal to teach enslaved Africans to read and write in the South – 5% became literate at great personal risk!" I also added a note in the margins about the North and South beginning to demonstrate disparate views on the topic of education to maintain slavery.

Panel Text:

- 1651 – John Eliot, Missionary, Natick, MA – Native residents taught to read and write in native language – Massachusett, using Roman alphabet.
- While some schools in the North allowed both Native and African Americans to attend, the main purpose was assimilation and religious indoctri-

"Early schooling was intended to produce youth who would obey and could read the BIBLE. Corporal punishment was intended to drive the DEVIL from the child's body."

nation. 1703 – 1st Anglican Black School – NY..

Your Research Notes

I wonder what kinds of reactions you have to the paintings based on *The New England Primer*? Can you imagine being one of the children in the painting or one of the children left out? What thoughts would you have written down if you were painting this panel?

Possible Actions

We are establishing patterns – frameworks for responding to the panels. You can add to these frameworks and create your own. It might be that you like the idea of beginning with a conversation about who should decide what curriculum our children study? How can we ensure that all students are equally represented and see themselves as history makers? Once again, inspired by this radical idea, there's a role for all children and young people who are writers, devisers, rhymers, dancers, and of course, painters, to participate in restorative justice projects and activities, and for children from diverse communities to create new spaces for learning.

Indian Removal Act - 1830
• 15,665 people of Cherokee Nation memorialize Congress in PROTEST.
• Outraged citizens join to protest across U.S.
1838
Trail of Tears
Thousands died.
(Estimated 4,000+)

1864-Navajo Long Walk
Estimated 2,380 died.
8,500+ men, women, and children forced off their land - marched and held by military in internment camp for four years

“

We, the great mass of the people think only of the love we have for our land, we do love the land where we were brought up. We will never let our hold to this land go, to let it go it will be like throwing away (our) mother that gave (us) birth.” - Aitooweyah, Cherokee

PANEL FOUR: INDIAN REMOVAL - CHEROKEE TRAIL OF TEARS AND NAVAJO LONG WALK

Imagine for a moment you have painted the first three panels and you are trying to make sure you do not leave anyone out. I struggled with this. I wanted to make sure that in addition to the history of the immigrants, I painted images that authentically represented the suffering of Indigenous peoples who were forced to relinquish their land. This panel represents a small fraction of those killed, starved, infected with disease, or relocated to reservations far from their ancestral homelands. I knew when I was painting that I would be relying on you to complete the story by finding out as I did what happened to the Native Americans – if they survived their removal and journey. Troubled, I added notes.

My Research Notes in the Margins of the Fourth Panel

- The Cherokee resisted. They created their own newspaper called "The Cherokee Phoenix" spreading their views and sent an educated group of their young men on a speaking tour, across the U.S. They created a petition,

"This panel represents a small fraction of those killed, starved, infected with disease, or relocated to reservations far from their ancestral homelands."

gathering over 15,000 signatures. They moved their case to the Supreme Court, but President Jackson disregarded the case despite their win of Worcester vs Georgia.

- The Seminoles of Florida were also forcibly removed at this time.
- Chief Sequoyah developed the Cherokee alphabet in 1820. Within months much of the Cherokee nation was literate. preservation

Your Research Notes

Here are three questions. What kinds of reactions do you have to the paintings? Can you imagine yourself in the captor's role first, then as those marched at rifle and bayonet point along the Trail of Tears? What thoughts would you have written down if you were painting this panel?

Possible Actions

Beginning again with a conversation. Black Elk, an Oglala Sioux Holy Man who lived from 1863 to 1950 said, "*Everything an Indian does is in a circle, and that is because the Power of the World always works in circles, and everything tries to be round.*" You could begin by talking together about Black Elk's observation and asking yourselves how this idea creates opportunities for restorative justice and reconciliation. Once again there's a role for all writers, devisers, rhymers, dancers, and of course, painters, of every age to participate in creating new learning spaces for children from diverse communities.

Tom Turtino - After

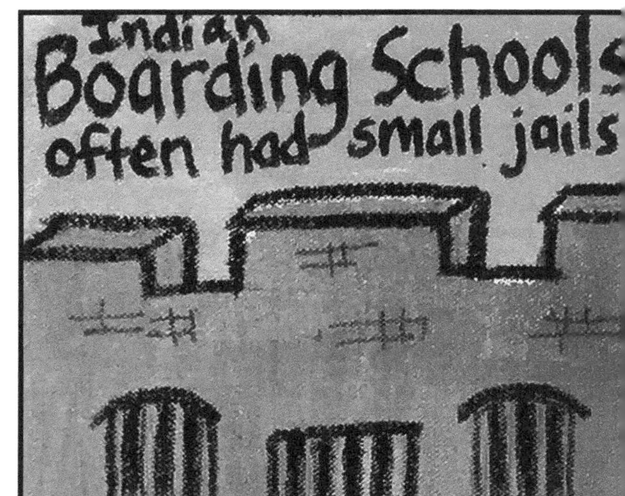
Indian
Boarding Schools
often had small jails

Indian
Boarding
Schools
used
abuse.

Navajo -
Befor

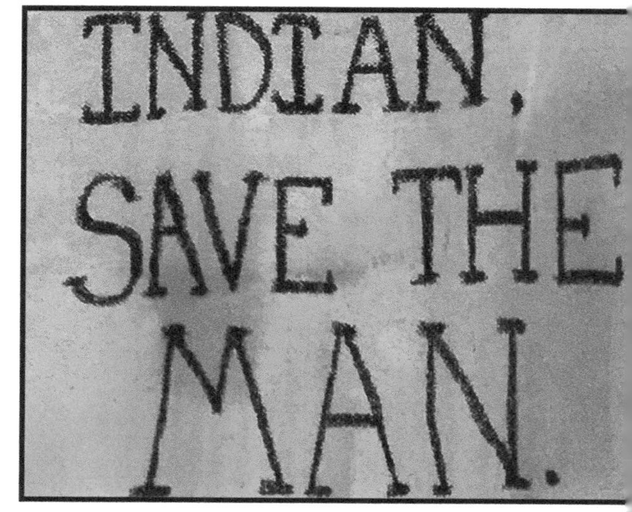
INDIAN,
SAVE THE
MAN.

“

The miseducation of American Indians precedes the ‘birth’ of this nation. From the time of invasion to the present day, the church and state have acted as coconspirators in the theft of Native America, robbing indigenous peoples of their very right to be indigenous.”
- Sandy Grande

PANEL FIVE: BOARDING SCHOOLS - AN ETHNIC CLEANSING

While painting this panel, I thought of Sandy Grande, who is the author of *Red Pedagogy – Native American Social and Political Thought*, and when I contemplated the next panel I was thinking about the above quote and the dogs that were sicced on Indigenous men, women and children who were peacefully protesting at Standing Rock in the summer of 2016. I wanted to paint authentic images of the trauma and shock experienced by Indigenous families when the U.S. military by order of the U.S. Government forcibly removed them from their land. I found myself painting the pain I felt in my heart as I thought of how they must have felt when their children were taken from them and confined in boarding schools where they were forced to speak English, relinquish their cultural heritage, and that were more like prisons or forced labor camps than schools.

My Research Notes in the Margins of the Fifth Panel

- The U.S. Military, Missionaries, and teachers acted with Congressional and Presidential orders to forcibly remove Native American children ages 6 to 16 and place them into Native/Indian Boarding Schools far from home to "Kill the Indian and save the man." This act was one of massive ethnic

> **" I wanted to paint authentic images of the trauma and shock experienced by Indigenous families when the U.S. military by order of the U.S. Government forcibly removed them from their land."**

cleansing.

- Carlisle School opened in 1879. There are 163 Bureau of Indian Affairs schools today.

Your Research Notes

Again, three questions. What kinds of reactions do you have to the paintings? Can you imagine being forcibly separated from your family and sent to a boarding school to eradicate your ethnic identity? What thoughts would you have written down if you were painting this panel?

Possible Actions

You might begin by reflecting on your previous conversations and how you would like to frame this discussion. Perhaps this is a moment when you feel comfortable talking about the idea that historically the U.S. government engaged in actions that today would be called "ethnic cleansing"? You might want to ask how these actions were morally justified and how these actions have impacted the lives of Indigenous people who have survived and are part of American society today. You might also find that your discussion has created an opportunity for you to reach out to Native Americans in your community and ask if they would like to join you in hosting a Restorative Justice Circle.

RSTUV
WXYZ
B
A

anized to
r children
brin

bring

12
+19
f
ne

rier
some
were
d.

ion
to the
e
South

“

The South believed an educated Negro to be a dangerous Negro. And the South was not wholly wrong; for education among all kinds of men always has had, and always will have, an element of danger and revolution, of dissatisfaction and discontent. Nevertheless, men strive to know.” - W.E.B. Du Bois

PANEL SIX: RECONSTRUCTION - BLACK RESISTANCE - THE FREEDMEN'S BUREAU

Thinking about the next panel I searched through the images I'd saved on my cell phone that I'd discovered in my research and studied them. It was a moment of hope and possibility that I knew would be quickly dashed. This panel would focus on the time when African Americans took a central role in creating U.S. public education. Africans brought to America as slaves were not allowed to learn to read, and freed slaves were forbidden from attending public schools. But there was a brief period when some schools were integrated, and I wanted to paint that hopeful moment when Black and white educators worked alongside one another for all their children, and in addition when they created normal schools for African Americans to receive training to become teachers. Colleges and universities for African Americans were formed that continue to lead today.

My Research Notes in the Margins of the Fifth Panel

- Post-Civil War – Reconstruction – Freedmen's Bureau opened 1,000 schools

"Africans brought to America as slaves were not allowed to learn to read, and freed slaves were forbidden from attending public schools. But there was a brief period when some schools were integrated."

serving 90,000 former slaves – and their children.

- Native Georgians, black and white, plus teachers from the North taught in these schools.
- 1/4 of Georgia's Freedmen School teachers were African American.
- The Freedmen's Bureau closed in 1870, and with little funding, about 10% of Georgia's African Americans could attend school during Reconstruction.
- Segregation became the law.

Your Research Notes

Once again, three questions. What kinds of reactions do you have to the paintings? Can you imagine what it was like for African Americans who were called "freed slaves" struggling to ensure their children could attend U.S. public schools, and what it must have been like when their schools became segregated? What thoughts would you have written down if you were painting this panel?

Possible Actions

I wonder if the experiences of discussing the history of Indigenous people have opened up possibilities for conversations about African Americans families who also struggled to make sure their children had an excellent public education. Your discussion might lead to an exploration of why it is important for families of color to have a voice in creating public school policies. Why do you think the NAACP is calling for a moratorium on charter schools? Again there's a role for all writers, devisers, rhymers, dancers, and of course, painters, of every age to participate in documenting the past and responding to the present social and institutional injustices experienced by African American families and their children attending U.S. public schools.

"Mexican Americans have lower levels of education than non-Hispanic Whites and Blacks. Some scholars have argued that this is a result of Mexican immigrants having relatively low levels of education especially by standards in the United States, yet this gap is persistan and continues into the fourth generation (Telles & Ortiz, 2008). To explair this, we have argued that the education disadvantage for Mexican Americans largely reflects their treatment as a stigmatized racial group rather than simply being a result of low immigrant human capital or of othe causes suggested in the literature. (Telles & Ortiz, 2008). -NCBI

Note: Mission schools most often resulted in cultural and linguistic genocide.

Common Schools moved West 1840-1850 - Public schools aided in cultural and linguistic genocide, clashing with the values of Mexican Americans.
Anglo parents often insisted on segregation to protect white children from being schooled with the "dirty and diseased." -NPS

“

Once social change begins, it cannot be reversed. You cannot un-educate the person who has learned to read. You cannot humiliate the person who feels pride. You cannot oppress the people who are not afraid anymore.” - Cesar Chavez

PANEL SEVEN: MEXICAN AMERICANS FIGHT ASSIMILATION

I continued to search and read historic documents, and I became deeply aware that there are narrative loops that many racial and ethnic groups share through institutional racism in U.S. public schools. I thought of Black Elk, the Oglala Sioux Holy Man who spoke of life occurring in circles, and the ways in which oppression and liberation can take place in recurring rounds – and I considered the ways in which these rounds unite the stories not only of Indigenous people and African slaves, but also Mexican immigrants and other persecuted groups who came to the U.S. thinking of it as the promised land. I knew that in this panel I wanted to inspire empathy for Mexican children and youth who were oppressed during this period of history, but I also wanted to expose how Mexican Americans also experienced broken treaties. And for this reason I chose to include a quote from Telles & Ortiz actually on the panel, but I still wrote notes in the margins.

My Research Notes in the Margins of the Fifth Panel

- 1846-1848 – After years of oppression via Spain – hostilities grew between Mexico and the U.S. Mexicans in the Southwest promised full rights as citizens in the Treaty of Guadeloupe-Hidalgo after the U.S.-Mexican War;

"I knew that in this panel I wanted to inspire empathy for Mexican children and youth who were oppressed during this period of history, but I also wanted to expose how Mexican Americans also experienced broken treaties."

but instead they became targets of oppression once again. During early statehood in Texas, Mexican children had no access to public schools. By the 1890's they had access to poorly funded segregated schools.

- Barrios began in the 1850's in So. California. Anglos were hostile to Mexican Americans outside the Barrios. The Barrios helped preserve Mexican culture in CA, reducing assimilation. Mexican segregated schools often only offered elementary education. Resistance was common, but mostly ineffective.

Your Research Notes

Again this is the moment when you are asked what kinds of reactions you have to the paintings. Can you imagine what it was like for Mexican American children who were treated as a stigmatized racial group in experiencing what Telles and Ortiz describe as "cultural and linguistic genocide" in U.S. public school? What thoughts would you have written down if you were painting this panel?

Possible Actions

In your collective groups you now have an opportunity to continue the conversation, perhaps considering the idea of recurring narrative loops in racism and discrimination experienced not only by Mexican American children and youth, but all the children whose experiences are documented in the panels you have discussed so far. It might be that this is the moment when you take up the idea of participating in "lessons in empathy" that Parkland student activist Emma González wrote of in a Tweet after visiting with Black high school students in Chicago. What an opportunity for writers, devisers, rhymers, dancers, and of course, painters, of every age to take the lead in creating lessons of empathy that can be shared on social media to reach out to all disenfranchised groups who have experienced social and institutional injustices in U.S. public schools.

Common Schools:
Horace Mann argued all citizens, regardless of race or economic status, shoul have equal access to a tuition-free, tax support public school system to achieve the unshackled status of a true DEMOCRACY. -
Boston State Univ.

• Texas Rangers Killed hundr -or thousands of Mexican Amer icans between 1915-1919.

• Lynching was common betwe 1860-1960, more than 4,000 African Americans were lynched between 1877-1950. Native Amer icans, Mexican Americans, and Asians were also lynched-as we as whites who helped Blacks.

Maintaining Oppression

Chinese Must Go!
• 1853 - Chinese children locked out of public edu-cation. 1st Presbyterian Church opens for them 1869. -Pressreader San Francisco
1927 - Gong Lum v. Rice Supreme Court rules Chinese as non-white for segregation in public schools.

“

Give me your tired, your poor,Your huddled masses yearning to breathe free, The wretched refuse of your teeming shore.Send these, the homeless, tempest-tost to me, I lift my lamp beside the golden door!” - Emma Lazarus

PANEL EIGHT: THE COMMON SCHOOL MOVEMENT AND "CHINESE MUST GO"

Painting the previous panels I constantly questioned whether the images I was creating presented an authentic view of the history of U.S. public schools. I kept thinking of Horace Mann, who was born in 1796 and lived until 1859, and was a lifelong advocate for all children to have equal access to public schools. I thought about the important roles white allies played to children of color in history as I painted Horace Mann. On the next panel you will find it juxtaposed with the lynching of both African and Mexican Americans. Recognizing too, how Asian Americans are often left out of current discussions on racism, I then focused on the history of Chinese American families and their children and the Chinese Exclusion Act of 1882. I then wrote on the panel that in 1927 the Supreme Court ruled that Chinese are non-white to justify the segregation of their children in U.S. public schools.

"Painting the previous panels I constantly questioned whether the images I was creating presented an authentic view of the history of U.S. public schools."

My Research Notes in the Margins of the Fifth Panel

- 1850 – 9 out of 10 adult white Americans can read and millions bought books written by the dominant culture.
- 1870 – 500 public schools, 50,000 students – mostly educating White boys – early grades only considered important for girls.
- 1882 – Chinese Exclusion Act, 39,500 immigrants in 1882, decreased to only 10 by 1887.

Your Research Notes

So much was happening at this time the three questions will give you an opportunity to frame your response to the panel. Here they are. What kinds of reactions do you have to the paintings, and also to my research notes? Can you imagine being Horace Mann advocating for equal access or a Chinese American child excluded from public schools? What thoughts would you have written down if you were painting these panels?

Possible Actions

In your discussions about this panel you might consider the "lessons in empathy" that Horace Mann inspires, but also how the ideals of the Horace Mann's Common School Movement conflicted with the Chinese Exclusion Act? In your discussions you might find the roles of the U.S. Government and the Supreme Court are difficult to ignore. What is extraordinary about this moment in time is that many young people are speaking out on the issues you are discussing, and your active engagement through social media provides so many opportunities for you as writers, devisers, rhymers, dancers, and painters, of every age to share your lessons in empathy on social media to hold the government accountable for institutional racism and social injustice in U.S. public schools.

1848 - 1st "Reform School" opens combining education with
juvenile justice system, beginning the school-t
prison pipeline still in effect today.
Unfortunately, this was neither a sc
nor did it "reform." It too
boys 7-17, mostly from sin
parent
homes.
-Lyman School for Boys 1885-1972
Lyman School for Boys Established 1848
JUVENILE COURT
1890
Sorting and ranking becomes widespread with the use of the BELL CURVE and implementation of grade levels & report cards.
- 1906 Nationality Act requires ability to speak English for naturalization.
- 1917 Immigration Act excluded illiterate from entering U.S.

“

Where justice is denied, where poverty is enforced, where ignorance prevails, and where any one class is made to feel that society is an organized conspiracy to oppress, rob and degrade them, neither persons nor property will be safe.” - Frederick Douglass

PANEL NINE: THE BELL CURVE, JUVENILE JUSTICE AND THE SCHOOL TO PRISON PIPELINE

I knew as I contemplated the next panel that I had reached a point where I had two paths in front of me. So many people coming to America experienced discrimination. The Irish who came during the great potato famine – which resulted in the death of between 1,000,000 and 1,500,000 people in Ireland – suffered ethic discrimination in the U.S., while Jewish people fleeing the pogroms in Russia and Poland suffered religious discrimination. I could either paint panels to represent all the groups, or focus on some of the mechanisms by which racism and discrimination occurred. I chose the second path to encourage readers to delve more deeply into the policies that were put into place that are used in one form or another to maintain institutional racism in U.S. public schools. Studying images, I painted the first reform school and flagged the juvenile court, then added the Bell Curve, which is now regarded by many psychologists and mathematicians as a totally discredited way of representing human abilities. Racism continued to dominate, but discrimination against many other ethnic and religious groups was prevalent. I crammed the margins with the findings of my research, keeping the panels focused on the policies and laws that were institutionalized in US public schools.

My Research Notes in the Margins of the Fifth Panel

- 1899 – Supreme Court allows a state to levy taxes on Black and white citizens alike while providing a public school for white children only. (Cumming v. Richmond, (GA) County Board of Education).
- 1893 – Mandatory education for Indian children in Boarding Schools –

"Racism continued to dominate, but discrimination against many other ethnic and religious groups was prevalent."

Native language forbidden. If parents refused, annuities or rations could be withheld or send them to jail. Educators had quotas to fill. Many died at school.

- 1913 – U.S. v. Sandoval, Supreme Court, American Indians "simple, uninformed & inferior people" – incapable of citizenship.

Your Research Notes

Again, what kinds of reactions do you have to the paintings, and also to my research notes? Many of you will not need to imagine being evaluated on the highly contentious Bell Curve because you will have experienced it. Given that fact, what research notes would you have written if you were painting these panels?

Possible Actions

The shift in this panel to a focus on the mechanisms used by policy makers to institutionalize racism and discrimination in U.S. public schools raises the possibility of many actions for you to consider. One action already underway is the Opt Out Movement, which takes on added significance given the depiction in the paintings. You might begin by asking, even if all children received an equal opportunity to a public education, what human qualities and achievements cannot be measured and represented on the Bell Curve? For example, in many communities across America young people are taking a leadership role in response to gun violence, including the racial profiling of Black shootings by police and the mass shootings in our schools. If we listed these student activists' attributes based on our observations of their extraordinary efforts we would include: creativity, critical thinking, resilience, motivation, persistence, curiosity, endurance, reliability, enthusiasm, empathy, self-awareness, self-discipline, leadership, civic-mindedness, courage, compassion, resourcefulness, sense of beauty, sense of wonder, honesty, and integrity. One of the students at Marjory Stoneman Douglas High School, Cameron Kasky comes to mind, who said, "Welcome to the revolution" when he advocated for young people to use their voices to "create a better world for generations to come." What actions would make a difference and become the focus of your own efforts – as writers, devisers, rhymers, dancers, and painters, of every age?

EUGENICS
GENETICS
ANTHROPOLOGY
STATISTICS
TESTING
HISTORY
GEOLOGY
ARCHEOLOGY
ETHNOLOGY
GEOGRAPHY
LAW

“

“We hold these truths to be self-evident, that all men are created equal, that they are endowed by their Creator with certain unalienable rights, that among these are life, liberty, and the pursuit of happiness.”
- The Declaration of Independence

PANEL TEN: SEGREGATION AND EUGENICS

Painting the panels became even more complicated when I reached the end of the Nineteenth Century and the beginning of the 20th Century. I studied the policies and laws put into place that cemented institutional racism and discrimination in U.S. public schools, and I wondered how to represent both the abstract ideas of Eugenics and segregation as well their very real impact on children and youth directly impacted in U.S. public schools. I thought of how equality and the unalienable rights to pursue life, liberty and happiness disappeared, and that when the curtain was pulled back it revealed that these rights were truly intended for only rich white men, reminding me of the oligarchs of today. I thought about Eugenics, standardized testing, and re-segregation – post Abolition and Reconstruction – and I connected these mechanisms to the institutionalizing of both racism and capitalism. Eugenicists used biased standardized tests and schools to rank order human beings, in order to try to prove that skin color, disabilities, physical and other visual differences, were linked to intelligence – then making decisions to stigmatize, institutionalize, and sterilize people based on these differences. I knew it was important and I did my best to represent this, but before I began I added research notes in the margins.

My Research Notes in the Margins of the Fifth Panel

- 1905 – 1st IQ tests by Alfred Binet used in Eugenics to discriminate and

"I thought about Eugenics, standardized testing, and re-segregation - post Abolition and Reconstruction - and I connected these mechanisms to the institutionalizing of both racism and capitalism."

prove "white supremacy."

- Scientific racism is used even today via high stakes testing to function as rationalization for white privilege and inequality. In *Ethical Technology*, Benjamin Abbott (2013) writes "Inequality requires rank ordering."

Your Research Notes

Again, what reactions do you have to the paintings, and also to my painted thoughts? Segregation continues today and your thoughts on this are important, similarly about Eugenics and the implications for American society of this heinous aspect of U.S. history. What thoughts would you have written down if you were painting these panels?

Possible Actions

Conversations about Eugenics might be difficult and disturbing, nevertheless your efforts to share your thoughts and feelings are important. More accessible for possible actions is the use of high stakes standardized tests, which continue to exclude racial and ethnic groups and *all* children who are poor and living in poverty. These tests are not only scientifically indefensible, but also socially unfair, unjust, and undemocratic. You might decide this is the issue on which your discussion group could unite with other groups by joining to defend students' and parents' rights to Opt Out of high stakes testing. By working together across racial, ethnic and religious groups and by crossing class lines you empower yourselves, and you can empower other people directly. You might decide that this is the moment to join with others in organizing a town meeting or a protest march. If so, there is a leadership role for your writers, devisers, rhymers, dancers, and painters, in imagining a collective action that brings hope and possibility through your music, poetry and art.

CRACY
kefeller

Rockefeller
and Carnegie,
like Bill Gates
Eli Broad, and
Waltons, Kochs
used their wea
to radically be
the public educ
system in ways
sort, rank, and
children of color
Carnegie

MERITOCRACY
TECHNOCRACY
PHILANTHROPY

SCHOOL
$

Ro
ar
lik
El
Wa
usec
to r
the
Carne

TEC
Technocracy
PHILAN

“

Leaders who do not act dialogically, but insist on imposing their decisions, do not organize the people - they manipulate them. They do not liberate, nor are they liberated: they oppress.” - Paulo Freire

PANEL ELEVEN: THE PHILANTHRO-CAPITALISTS

Sometimes when contemplating a panel, there were uncanny moments when I had a sense of being inside the scene. They say history repeats. True. Again I thought of Black Elk's circles and rounds, and their use today with the concept of narrative loops. I knew this panel on philanthro-capitalists would carry forward to the time in which we now live. The evidence is indisputable. The great wealth of Carnegie and Rockefeller was earned through neglect of and brutality to workers. I could feel the weight of history on my shoulders as I contemplated the images I was going to paint. My brush became the way in which I expressed my disgust and sorrow at the ways in which these philanthro-capitalists used their wealth and power to institutionalize public school policies that increased the use of Eugenics and standardized tests to separate, segregate, and to exclude children and their families. They created a phony "meritocracy" to track and sort people to increase their profits and their immense wealth. I wrote my research notes in the margins.

My Research Notes in the Margins of the Eleventh Panel

- 1912 –Began 1st mass use of IQ tests at Ellis Island – immigration.
- 1932 – Survey of 150 school districts reveals ¾ of them use "so-called" IQ

"My brush became the way in which I expressed my disgust and sorrow at the ways in which these philanthro-capitalists used their wealth and power to institutionalize public school policies that increased the use of Eugenics and standardized tests to separate, segregate, and to exclude children and their families."

testing to place students into different academic tracks.

- 1947 – Educational Testing Service (ETS) is formed – merges with College Entrance Examination Board, Cooperative Test Service, Graduate Records Office, National Committee on Teachers Examinations and Carnegie Foundations and continued to work directly with Eugenicists like Carl Brigham (originator of SAT) to prove immigrants were "feeble minded".

Your Research Notes

Again three questions. What reactions do you have to the paintings – does it seem like déjà vu to you? Can you imagine arriving at Ellis Island and your first experience on arrival being required to pass an I.Q. test as a contingency for being accepted into the United States, or a child tracked and excluded from learning opportunities in public school? What thoughts would you have written down if you were painting these panels?

Possible Actions

Your conversation might begin with your responses to the panels – which I admit I find disturbing even though I painted them – because it is such a reflection on what is happening at the present time. You might want to discuss the propaganda techniques used by the philanthro-capitalists of the past and the current ones today, and you might decide to follow up by discussing how Lewis Terman still influences public education and perpetuates institutional racism today. It might be that you hold tight on the issues you have discussed and wait until you discuss panel 17 on the philanthro-capitalists who are having a negative impact on U.S. public schools today.

oy" could
ecome a
langer.
46 – Mendez
Westminster
segregates
LIFORNIA
exican
nericans
49 –

aring
egation
blic
ol children
54
own v.
oard of Ed

suits over unequal pay for
acks and whites in South.
3 – NAACP begins legal
mpaign to desegregate
ucation.
5 – SC requires school
drivers to be same
e as students.
5 – Southern
nsensus – "An

could
e a
er.
Mendez
rminster
egates
RNIA

CALIFORNIA
Mexican
Americans
1949 –
17 states
enacted

“

Each and every one of us is born with a clean heart. Our babies know nothing about hate or racism. But soon they begin to learn - and only from us. We keep racism alive. We pass it on to our children. We owe it to our children to help them keep their clean start.” - Ruby Bridges

PANEL TWELVE: RUBY BRIDGES

I was shaken by the feelings of disgust I experienced as I compared Ruby Bridge's "clean heart" quote to the unscrupulous oligarchs who put into place the institutional practices that segregated, separated, and excluded children from equal access to high quality learning opportunities. I kept asking "where's the hope?" and in that moment I decided that the next panel would depict the courageous efforts of African Americans who responded to the injustices they were forced to endure. I knew that 1930 through 1960 was a turbulent time, and that many Black families participated in the struggle for integration and equity in public schools. Studying various images I decided to illustrate the courageous path walked by 6-year-old Ruby Bridges. Ruby was escorted by U.S. marshals to protect her from violence as the first Black child to attend the all-white William Frantz Elementary School in Louisiana. As a kindergarten teacher of many young Black children, I thought of Ruby who was forced to take an intelligence test to be allowed integration as a kindergartner. This was not without risk to Ruby or her family. Deep in the segregated South, parents could be fined and imprisoned for attempting desegregation. Close to tears and feeling angry, but also with a sense of hope, I painted Ruby and wrote a chronology of the Black struggle in the South. I included Brown v Board of Education, and out of room I once again wrote in the margins of the panel.

"This was not without risk to Ruby or her family. Deep in the segregated South, parents could be fined and imprisoned for attempting desegregation. Close to tears and feeling angry, but also with a sense of hope, I painted Ruby and wrote a chronology of the Black struggle in the South."

My Research Notes in the Margins of the Twelfth Panel

- Despite Brown v Board of Education, Louisiana amended their Constitution to require segregation. Penalty: $500-$1,000 and prison 3-6 months.
- Most Southern states defied the Supreme Court, "Massive Resistance" unleashed.

Your Research Notes

This time there are more than three questions but they are essentially the same. First what reactions do you have to the panel? How would you have responded if you had been Ruby? Her mother? The U.S. marshals? The white students? Their parents? Lawmakers? The President? What notes would you have written if you were painting the panel?

Possible Actions

By now your conversations about possible actions will have taken a quantum leap beyond our most radical of radical imaginations! In the aftermath of the mass shooting at Marjory Stoneman Douglas High School, students who survived the massacre joined hands with students from Chicago, Virginia, and communities across the U.S. to lead the nation and the global community in mass demonstrations for gun control laws so that no more children and young people are killed in or out of school. But this is not the first time children took serious matters into their own hands. In 1963 children climbed over school fences to protest racism, and while "Bull" Connor turned fire hoses and dogs on them, they too joined hands to form a human chain of strength. The tide in civil rights movement turned that day, just as the tide is turning because the students of Margery Stoneman Douglas, Black Lives Matter and Standing Rock refuse to remain victims. Possible actions are no longer hypothetical, and mass demonstrations on a global scale can happen where everyone has an opportunity to participate.

Most of the
removed for
adults
Years of

IS RACISM!
But
ill Make IT
POORER
Little Rock Nine
NAACP

NAACP

removed for 'national
children,
and young
adults not yet

“

“We saw all these people behind the fence, looking out, hanging onto the wire, and looking out because they were anxious to know who was coming in. But I will never forget the shocking feeling that human beings were behind this fence like animals [crying]. And we were going to also lose our freedom and walk inside of that gate and find ourselves cooped up there when the gates were shut, we knew that we had lost something that was very precious; that we were no longer free.” - Mary Tsukamoto

PANEL THIRTEEN: JAPANESE INTERNMENT, EMMETT TILL, AND THE LITTLE ROCK NINE

I have become conscious that you are viewing the panels after the national and global protest on gun violence in American and the mass shootings in U.S. public schools. It is a step change in the U.S. psyche and the largest protest in America's history. But vigilance is still essential, for while the narrative has changed, old narratives still exist and inevitably will reoccur. In the summer of 2017 there was not even a glimmer of these thoughts in my mind. What I felt was the tension between the negative actions of the powerful and privileged, and the courage and determination of people to change the future for their children. I looked for images of school-age children behind barbed wire fences while they hold their hands to their hearts in the Pledge of Allegiance to the United States of America, and I imagined what it must have been like for them and their parents in their confusion, deep hurt and shame. My thoughts turned to the brutal murder of Emmett Till who I painted next to Ruby Bridges. I mourned the loss of the unfulfilled potential I sense in Emmett Till's kind and intelligent eyes, and once again I fought back tears as I thought about how many innocent young Black people have been killed in recent years. But I didn't want to leave this time without remembering the courage of the Little Rock Nine, who were a group of nine Black students who enrolled at formerly all-white Central

"But vigilance is still essential, for while the narrative has changed, old narratives still exist and inevitably will reoccur."

High School in Little Rock, Arkansas, in September 1957. I thought of so many children, so many voices of young people, some lost, some heard, some strong and fighting for justice as I wrote my research notes in the margins of the panel.

My Research Notes in the Margins of the Thirteenth Panel

- 1955 – 14-year-old Chicago teen murdered in Mississippi. His murderers are acquitted. Emmett Till had attended a segregated school in Chicago. His brutal murder lit a spark in the Civil Rights Movement.
- 1956 – NAACP barred from Alabama.
- 1957 – Eisenhower sends U.S. Army 1,200-man 327th Battle Group to Little Rock, Arkansas to take control of Central High School, plus 10,000 National Guardsmen. The Little Rock Nine began attending classes 9-25-1957.

Your Research Notes

By now I don't need to write the three questions. You know them. What is your response to the panels? Can you imagine being a Japanese youth being imprisoned and forced to pledge allegiance to the U.S. flag? Or being a Black child when 12,200 troops descending on Little Rock, Arkansas? Or, a member of the family of Emmett Till getting the news of his lynching? Trayvon Martin's or Tamir Rice's family? What thoughts would you have written down?

Possible Actions

Perhaps in your discussion you might want to begin with the idea "together we will be strong" that was Tweeted by Emma González, and that even though other school shootings have now taken place, and the national and global March For Our Lives rally against gun violence that followed the Parkland massacre is now part of our shared history – together we will be strong. "We are here for you, students of Great Mills," Emma tweeted, "together we can stop this from ever happening again." Finally, in your creative and radical imaginings, is there a way for your writers, devisers, rhymers, dancers, and painters, to organize collective actions that unite us whatever our race, gender, ethnicity, or place of origin, and that bring hope and possibility when events take place that take or threaten the lives of young people through your music, poetry and art?

SCHOOL

"National Tragedy" repor
merican Boarding Schools. B
ys he still has nightmares
busive discipline and that he a

“

“Freedom is a seven letter word with great meaning. To many people, and myself, it is one of the greatest words when we are actually free. What I mean by free is to go to any place you want to without being involved in violence and being able to speak as you please.”
Larry B., 8th Grade, age 13 - Freedom School

PANEL FOURTEEN: FREEDOM SUMMER AND A NATIONAL TRAGEDY

Time was running out. I knew if the panels were to be ready for the BAT Conference I would have to paint quickly. I kept thinking of the tensions I'd been documenting in the panels between hope and tragedy, and immediately I knew that the next panel would be a depiction of the young African American girls in the Freedom School who appear so confident in the images I was studying on my cell phone, and also knew I would contrast their smiling faces with the images I was looking at of the children in a Native American boarding school who had been taken from their families to be assimilated into the dominant white Christian culture. I realized time and space didn't allow me to tell the whole story, and so after I had painted the pictures I uncapped another new marker and wrote "1964 CIVIL RIGHTS ACT" which came just a few years before the publication of the 1969 Report, *A National Tragedy – A National Challenge* was released. Still there was more I wanted to convey and so once again I added my research notes.

My Research Notes in the Margins of the Fourteenth Panel

- 1964 – LBJ signs Civil Rights Act – Prohibits SEGREGATION and financial

"I kept thinking of the tensions I'd been documenting in the panels between hope and tragedy, and immediately I knew that the next panel would be a depiction of the young African American girls in the Freedom School."

support to any institution or agency promoting Jim Crow.

- 1964 – Freedom Summer (CORE and SNCC), Algebra Project founder Bob Moses, MS and HS students taught art of resistance and protest. UFT NY sends contingent, 2,500 students, insisted white educators include African American History in curriculum. These schools exist across country today, but goals have not been reached.
- 1966 – Bobby Seale and Huey Newton draft Ten Point Program for Black Panther Party, by the end of 1969 Black Panthers "served daily FREE breakfasts to 20,000 children across 19 cities.

Your Research Notes

Again, what is your response to the panels? Can you imagine attending a Freedom School to feel empowered and liberated, or a boarding school to be incarcerated and feel imprisoned and stripped of your cultural identity? What thoughts would you have written down?

Possible Actions

In your discussions you might begin by asking: Where are we now? What's happening today that might change the racist and discriminatory practices that are institutionalized in U.S. public schools? How are students mobilizing and marching to disrupt the structures of inequality? And when David Hogg, a senior at Marjory Stoneman Douglas High School, where a gunman shot and killed 17 people, calls out the media for unequal coverage of gun violence against Black and Brown youth, how can we respond to that? Hogg shared the powerful intersectionality we saw on stage on March 24th 2018 in D.C.'s March for Our Lives, stating, "We have to use our white privilege now to make sure that all of the people that have died as a result of [gun violence] and haven't been covered the same can now be heard." David Hogg, Emma Gonzalez, Alex Wind, Jaclyn Corin, Ryan Deitsch and Cameron Kasky are calling on all people regardless of race, ethnicity, gender or religion to unite – we are all one family – to end not only gun violence but also racism and discrimination. How can we all seize the moment in actions undertaken together for freedom, liberty and justice for all?

Valerie Banks was the ONLY student to show up on 1st day of geography at South Boston HS.
1974
Whites RIOT & Boycott rather than integrate

1974 Boston Riots over forced bussing, integration
The City has NO CLASSROOM FOR My Child

1971 - Ten school buses bombed by KKK - Pontiac, MI

forced bussing, forced integration was met with violence, massive resistance
STOP

"When we speak we are afraid our words will not be heard or welcomed. But when we are silent we are still afraid. So it is better to speak." - Audre Lorde

PANEL FIFTEEN: THE KKK AND THE INDIAN CHILD WELFARE ACT

I remember standing in front of the space on the canvas where I was about to paint the next panel, but my attention was focused on the images of children dressed in KKK hoods, and I thought about the many ways children are indoctrinated into racist attitudes and beliefs. Just as the NRA does now, the KKK silenced resistance through fear, which is not surprising given the historic connections between the KKK and the NRA. In the 1970's the KKK used violence, murder, and acts of sheer terror to maintain oppression and segregation in U.S. public schools. As I painted I thought about the history of the 2nd Amendment and its intent of keeping guns out of the hands of Blacks and in the hands of the slave patrols. Today the Neo-Nazis and white supremacists carry on the work of the KKK, and their connections are still evident with the NRA. The brutal violence of that time still exists, and the struggle continues in society and in U.S. public schools. One sign of hope I wanted to paint was the 1978 Indian Child Welfare Act, which finally returned the right to Indigenous parents to refuse to place their children in Native American Boarding Schools. I painted many images on this panel but still needed to write notes around the edges of the paintings.

My Research Notes in the Margins of the Fifteenth Panel

- 1970 – Whites attack African American school children by the school bus

"One sign of hope I wanted to paint was the 1978 Indian Child Welfare Act, which finally returned the right to Indigenous parents to refuse to place their children in Native American Boarding Schools."

load in Lamar, SC.

- 1971 – Ku Klux Klan dynamites 10 empty school buses, Pontiac, MI. Judge William Douglas rules Brown v. Board applies to Chinese Americans.
- 1973 – Black Panther School opens, serves kids 3meals/day – Oakland ruled "model for education that was replicable anywhere."
- 1975 – NAACP Marches in support of integration, busing, Boston.
- 1978 – Native Americans gain legal rights to DENY their own children's placement in off-reservation boarding schools, as intended these schools resulted in cultural genocide, broke parent-child sacred bond.

Your Research Notes

By now I am sure you are critically conscious of your response to the panels before I ask the questions. I wonder what connections you are making between these historical events connected to gun violence in poor urban communities and mass shootings in U.S. public schools today? What movements do you see that could possibly benefit from joining together to increase their success in common struggles for justice? And lastly, what thoughts would you have written down?

Possible Actions

You might consider starting off your conversation by talking about the Audre Lorde quotation. As I read now, I think about the silence used by Emma González during her March for Our Lives speech. Do you know of silence being used strategically in other protests? I expect like me there have been times when you have spoken up and been afraid nobody has heard you, or your words have not been welcome. But silence? What are the consequences of silence? That might be a good question to ask. The NRA went to great lengths to produce vile and threatening videos to silence the survivors of the mass shooting at Marjory Stoneman Douglas High School, but the students responded in ways that silenced the NRA. Knowing that there are historical connections between the NRA, the KKK and slavery, are there ways your writers, devisers, rhymers, dancers, and painters could use their talents and skills to organize a collective action?

2001-
No Child Left Behind

2005- "I think the best thing that happened to the education system in New Orleans was Hurricane Katrina." - Arne Duncan, US Sec. of Ed.
TAKE-OVER BY R S D
"No Excuses" Charter Schools
No textbooks, desks
Microwaved frozen meals,
Militarized Security outnumbering TEACHERS.
SCHOOL BUS

2009- Race
REWARD
Trauma
Biased Testing
Biased Curriculum
Poverty

“

Standardized tests have become the most effective racist weapon ever devised to objectively degrade Black minds and legally exclude their bodies.” - Ibram X. Kendi

PANEL SIXTEEN: NO CHILD LEFT BEHIND AND A RACE TO THE TOP - FOR WHOM?

The first fifteen panels tracing the history of institutional racism and discrimination leave little doubt that events taking place today should be suspect – including No Child Left Behind, President Obama's Race to the Top, and even the Every Child Succeeds Act. I studied many images, but chose an image of President George W. Bush in a photo-op with some little children. The President seems perplexed as he looks at the children and he is quoted as blaming low test scores and school closures on the "soft bigotry of low expectations." Bush avoided the opportunity to take economic and social responsibility, or to hold the government accountable for putting into place and maintaining conditions of inequality in U.S. public schools, instead blaming teachers, children and their families. He ignored the barriers to opportunity and seemed to not know that trauma studies have proven the long-term effects on the generations of those who are oppressed. The impact of laws to make it a crime to teach a slave to read, policies of exclusion, Eugenics, segregation, discrimination, under funding, sorting, ranking, corporal punishment, closing schools in predominantly Black and Brown neighborhoods in order to open charter schools for profit, all make the deception of No Child Left Behind, Race to the Top and Every Child Succeeds ignoble acts and crimes.

My Research Notes in the Margins of the Sixteenth Panel

- 1990's – Group of Chinese American educators demand Asian Americans not be "mere sidebars in text books."
- 1994 – Proposition 187 passes, California – undocumented immigrants

"Bush avoided the opportunity to take economic and social responsibility, or to hold the government accountable."

may NOT attend public school.

- 1996 – Milton Friedman launches the Friedman Foundation of Educational Choice, begins the siphoning of tax dollars from public schools into private hands. Controversy over Ebonics in public schools.
- 1998 – California breaks treaty with Proposition 227, making it illegal for teachers to speak Spanish in public schools.
- Goals 2000 – Standards Movement begins.
- 2001-02 – No Child Left Behind begins high-stakes testing to sort, rank, and cull students, educators, and close public schools based on standardized testing with roots deeply embedded in racism.
- 2005 – "No Excuse" Charters replace 119 NOLA public schools after Katrina.
- 2009 – Race to the Top raises the stakes, increasing the gap.

Your Research Notes

So – what are your responses to the panels? What have you discovered about No Child Left Behind, Race to the Top and Every Child Succeeds? Does your research support Audre Lorde's "*The master's tools will never dismantle the master's house*"? How would you hold the government accountable for putting into place and maintaining conditions of inequality in U.S. public schools? What research notes would you have written down?

Possible Actions

You could begin your discussion with a conversation about how hundreds of years of institutional racism and discrimination in U.S. public schools convinced many civil rights organizations to agree with Bush that children who lived in poor urban and rural poverty – Black, Brown and white – were victims of "the soft bigotry of low expectations". In fact, NCLB high stakes tests exacerbated the problem of educational inequities by disregarding the impact of poverty on children's lives, and by ignoring the moral and ethical responsibilities of the Federal and state governments to economic accountability as a key factor in the struggle for justice for all children attending U.S. public schools. By now you have many ways to respond in your toolbox to advocate for racial and economic justice. Your next step might be to decide what actions to take together.

SCHOOL SURVEILLANCE
PRIVATE
Hands Up! Don't Shoot!
PRISON PREP SCHOOL
ZERO TOLERANCE CHARTER
PUBLIC SCHOOL
SBA
Library Closed Testing
Segregated
Silenced
Surveilled
Suppressed
BANK
TAX HAVEN
TAX HAVEN

I trust that every animal here appreciates the sacrifice that Comrade Napoleon has made in taking this extra labour upon himself. Do not imagine, comrades, that leadership is a pleasure! On the contrary, it is a deep and heavy responsibility. No one believes more firmly than Comrade Napoleon that all animals are equal. He would be only too happy to let you make your decisions for yourselves. But sometimes you might make the wrong decisions, comrades, and then where should we be?" - George Orwell

PANEL SEVENTEEN: PHILANTHRO-CAPITALISTS EDTECH AND THE EYE OF SAURON

I remember standing looking at my drawing of this panel knowing that it was the best I could do to represent what's happening in our underfunded, over-policed, school-to-prison public schools. As I began to paint I thought about Bush, Clinton, Obama and now Trump, and how we were duped. I kept thinking that in a dystopian world created by the philanthro-capitalists we have to uncover the ways in which we support these elites by allowing them to maintain their power, control, and wealth. The propaganda sounds good: "Common Core," "college and career ready", "innovative schools", "personalized learning", "pathways", "safe schools", and "competing in the global market". Before the philanthro-capitalists used their white privilege to re-purpose public education by invigorating racist and discriminatory practices and sapping creativity and innovation, teachers used to ask young people to read challenging literature, and the arts and humanities were valued, because they had the potential to

"As I began to paint I thought about Bush, Clinton, Obama and now Trump, and how we were duped. I kept thinking that in a dystopian world created by the philanthro-capitalists we have to uncover the ways in which we support these elites by allowing them to maintain their power, control, and wealth."

transform lives. But today it's all about mandated Student Learning Objectives, standards, and citing pseudo text-based evidence. My concern for accurately representing this time is indicated by the masses of research notes I wrote.

My Research Notes in the Margins of the Seventeenth Panel

- 2008 – Bill Gates admits his small schools project was a failure. He neglected to admit school/community disruption, conflicts, students and teachers jumping ship en masse, and plummeting attendance, test scores, and graduation rates. SUMMER 2008 – Gene Wilhoit convinces Bill Gates to back Common Core.
- 2009 – Eli Broad releases "School Closure Guide – Closing Schools as a Means for Addressing Budgetary Challenges." 2009 – Stanford University's study finds 83% of all charter schools perform worse or no better than traditional public schools.
- 2010 – Arizona bans class on Mexican American studies – Activists Curtis Acosta, Tony Diaz, Jose Lara fight back, spread Ethnic Studies. Arne Duncan heads up Chicago's Renaissance 2010 Plan – creating military academy-like schools, expanding draconian expulsions, instituting high student surveillance, increasing police presence, shut down schools, fired entire school staffs, calling for 100's of school closures in poor, mostly Black neighborhoods – some Latino – private charter schools set up to replace.
- 2012 – Mayor Rahm Emanuel tells Chicago Teachers Union President "25% of the students in this city are never going to amount to anything and he is never going to throw money at it."
- 2013 – Boston University economics professors Olesya Baker & Kevin Lang's 2013 study: "The School to Prison Pipeline Exposed" reveals that increased use of high stakes standardized exit exams are inked to higher incarceration rates.
- 2014 – "Death by a Thousand Cuts" – Journey for Justice Alliance.
- 2014 – Baltimore Algebra Project stages die-in protesting school closures.
- 2014 – 5,000 opt out of state test in Colorado.
- 2015 – In New York, the number of Black students rated "below standard" jumped from 15.5% to 50% with the introduction of the new Common

Core tests. English learners did even worse. 84% tested "below standard" on the new tests.

- 2015 – 200,000 in New York opt out of state test.
- 2015 – 100s of a 90% Latino population in New Mexico organize mass walkouts protesting PARCC tests. 2015 – Newark Student Union occupied district headquarters in part to resist new Common Core tests, saying, "the Opt Out movement is a vital component of the Black Lives Matter movement... Using standardized tests to label Black people and immigrants 'lesser,' while systematically underfunding their schools, has a long and ugly history in this country."
- 2015 – Seattle King County NAACP takes position against Smarter Balanced Assessments and for the Opt Out movement.
- 2016 – Since its founding, Walton Family Foundation has given more than $1.3 billion to K-12 education...an amount that is surpassed only by the Bill and Melinda Gates Foundation. The Foundation's recent annual report shows well over 50% of its 2014 grantee investments went to education, $202 million out of $373 million.
- 2017 – Lawyers say Arizona's Ethnic Studies ban is Discriminatory, Illegal.

Your Research Notes

What is your response to this panel? There's an awful lot going on! How have things changed since the time of Rockefeller and Carnegie? How are they the same? How does the panel challenge the motto of Bill and Melinda Gates, which is "All lives have equal value." What thoughts would you have written down?

Possible Actions

We've come a long way from the first panel on the beginning of racism and discrimination in U.S. public schools. Few would argue that this is an incredible time when young people are setting the political agenda and establishing new priorities for social justice. Do you feel empowered to make a difference in the world? We are strong and we know we can make a difference in the world. Watch the stunning performance by Andra Day and Common at the People's State of the Union. Be inspired by the artists performing that night. By learning through identity politics, we are beginning to build bridges across movements and developing the necessary intersectionality of people to end the power of oligarchs. There is new hope and much to do together. Now is the time for you as writers, devisers, rhymers, dancers, and painters to use your talents and skills to organize further collective action.

Detroit Kindergarten Hub
DETROIT Kindergarten HUB
Personalized Learning
BOOK SHELF
MATH MANIPULATIVES
BLOCKS and
BOOK SHELF
SCIENCE EXPLORATION
DRAMATIC
LEAKS
We Shall Overcome
TRASH

"

Sixty years since Brown v. Board of Education, the school-to-prison pipeline continues to play a role in denying Black people their human right to an education, and privatization strips Black people of the right to self-determine the kind of education their children receive. This systematic attack is coordinated by an international education privatization agenda, bankrolled by billionaire philanthropists such as Bill and Melinda Gates, the Walton Family, and Eli and Edythe Broad, and aided by the departments of Education at the federal, state, and local level."- Jonathan Stith, Hiram Rivera, Chinyere Tutashinda

PANEL EIGHTEEN: THE SOFT BIGOTRY OF EDTECH AND "PERSONALIZED LEARNING"

I approached this final panel as a kindergarten teacher as well as an artist. I heard about the very real Kindergarten Hub in Detroit and was sickened. This painting is an imagining taken from what's happening in schools across America, but mostly from Detroit's Kindergarten Hub. The dystopian training-workers model of early childhood education is totally oppressive to early childhood teachers. We know the curriculum that is being imposed on children is harming their social as well as their academic development. Still more disturbing is that Black, Brown and all poor children are the ones who are the most impacted for years by the imposition by philanthro-capitalists of their "edtech", and by the policy makers who use their white privilege to maintain institutional racism in public schools. I wanted to paint this dystopian world in a way that would sound the alarm and expose the damage that is being done to kindergarten children. I settled on a scene in which five-year-olds have their eyes covered with virtual reality headsets transmitting the oligarchs' curriculum in 3-D, holding screens

"The dystopian training-workers model of early childhood education is totally oppressive to early childhood teachers. We know the curriculum that is being imposed on children is harming their social as well as their academic development."

that show only numbers, while books containing their history, art materials, blocks, and toys are disposed of in the trash. The move to socially restricting, active problem-solving limiting, physically restraining AI chat-bots, tablets, online learning, and so-called "personalized learning" is worthy of our serious concern, when healthy human relationships are what our society truly needs. Again, I wrote many research notes and key points are included here:

My Research Notes in the Margins of the Eighteenth Panel

- 2014 – Detroit, Michigan's Education Achievement Authority opens the "Kindergarten Hub" in a former school library. Class size is 100 kindergartners as a "low-cost" school model (experiment) based on "individualized" aka "Personalized Learning" – thus substituting computers for teachers. Meanwhile, Detroit's demographics include 82% or more Blacks, schools are in the death-throws of defunding shock doctrine, poverty is rampant. Conditions in one Detroit school inspired a student "cockroach killer" as a daily job, water is often unsafe, ceilings leak, rats populate classrooms, bathroom plumbing is in disrepair but kids get new laptops to "personalize" their learning. Meanwhile data is collected continually.
- 2017 – New study from Georgetown Center on Poverty and Equality finds adults view Black girls as less in need of protection than white girls ages 5-14.
- 2017 – Children of Standing Rock – Defenders of the Water School – founded by Alayna Eagle Shield. Sande Grande wrote "Children learned that the resistance was not just about a pipeline or even unchecked corporate power, but rather about their right to defend themselves, their land and relatives, including the Missouri River."

Your Research Notes

I hope that you have, like me, created your own questions and that you will pour over these images multiple times, but for now please consider for the last time in this book: What is your response to this panel? How do you feel about the removal of human interactions, play, art, literature, music, band, sports, and hands-on learning, and instead replacing these with a virtual reality screen?

What thoughts would you have written down?

Possible Actions

By now your conversations are deep and filled with insights on demonstrated ways of pushing back at the philanthro-capitalists and the policy makers who use their white privilege to maintain institutional racism and discrimination in public schools. We don't have to accept the oligarchs' worldview, nor their conditions. A key issue you might want to explore is the ways in which edtech, privatization, and personalized learning are being used to exacerbate institutional racism. On March 24th students and educators organized and marched across the nation, calling on the entire nation to make non-violence a way of life. One said, "We are not here to fight one another, we are all brothers and sisters." I was filled with hope when I began this project, and I feel even more hopeful now that we have reached the last page. We are empowered to create our own story of liberation, and to become the authors and the illustrators of our unshackled future together. Working across all racial, ethnic, religious and LGBTQ+ groups, participate with your writers, devisers, rhymers, dancers, and painters to advance intersectionality across movements to establish peaceful actions – letters, petitions, vigils, civil disobedience, marches, festivals, and artful resistance actions on social media using the hashtag #Act4EduJustice – for restorative justice and to protect all children in U.S. public schools.

ABOUT THE AUTHOR

SUSAN DUFRESNE

Susan DuFresne is an artist and educator who advocates across all intersectional groups, organizing for social justice. She works alongside colleagues and friends who are leaders in the Black Lives Matter Movement and the Badass Teachers Association. She is a vocal supporter of Indigenous peoples, the Women's Movement, and LGBTQIA activists, and cares deeply about environmental issues. She visualizes a future where these diverse groups join together to successfully return power to the people.

Susan is currently teaching children in an integrated kindergarten classroom as both a general education and special education teacher. She is active on social media and can often be found participating in marches and rallies for social justice locally and at the state and national levels. One of the important battles she fights is for democratically run schools, as well as a child's right to play. She pushes against the use of high stakes testing, agreeing with many students, parents, and educators who denounce these tests as racially biased, advocating for their right to opt out.

Susan and her husband live in Washington State. They have one son, three daughters and three grandchildren.

CPSIA information can be obtained
at www.ICGtesting.com
Printed in the USA
LVHW071027261219
641722LV00012B/209/P